Stephen

# NO ZEBRAS!

## *ENGAGING BYSTANDERS IN THE MOVEMENT TO END SEXUAL AGGRESSION*

*STEPHEN M. THOMPSON*
*No Zebras Productions, 1216 Clubhouse Drive, Lake Isabella, MI. 48893*

# No Zebras!

## *Engaging Bystanders in the Movement to End Sexual Aggression*

Copyright © 2020 Stephen M. Thompson

Stephen Thompson

# Table of Contents

# ACKNOWLEDGMENTS

This book has taken a career to complete. During those many years, I have had the privilege and opportunity to hear many voices that influenced me. First and foremost were the thousands of survivors voices; male, female, young and old. Each one with experiences that individually and collectively impacted me. The voices of family and friends of survivors who themselves were impacted as secondary survivors. The experiences and knowledge advocates throughout the country have shared with me. The written word and voices of the many experts in the field who have influenced my views and knowledge. The voices of law enforcement officers, prosecutors and judges who deal with the complexities of sexual aggression daily. Lastly, the written accounts as well as first hand interviews with the true experts in sexual aggression, the predators themselves. Collectively all these voices have influenced me in both a professional and personal way. Two more powerful people have been instrumental in bringing this book to completion. I am told one of my strengths is verbal communication through teaching, consulting, and presentations. Conversely, a major weakness is the fact that I write like I speak, which is not a plus. These two people have taken my ideas and words, making hundreds of editorial suggestions to improve the way this book is presented to the reader. My wife, Dr. Maureen MacGillivray used her experience as a published researcher as well as a very insightful woman, to suggest different ways to get my ideas across. The second is Ms. Rachel Wilson. Her experiences as a survivor coupled with her ability to write have had a

4

profound influence on the final product. To both, thank you. This book would not be completed nor would I be as proud of it without you.

"We told her not to wander off. What was she thinking? Let's get outta here!"

# A SURVIVOR 'S STORY

by Rachel Wilson

I f you've picked this book up, it is very likely that at some point in time either sexual violence or domestic violence has touched your life in some way. Maybe you've been directly impacted, or maybe someone you know or love is a survivor of sexual or domestic violence. If you just thought to yourself, "Neither of these apply to me," I would respectfully ask you to take a closer look and reconsider. According to the Centers for Disease Control, nearly 1 in 5 women and 1 in 7 men report having experienced severe physical violence from an intimate partner in their lifetime. More than 1 in 3 women and 1 in 8 men have experienced sexual violence involving physical contact during their lifetime. Chances are, someone close to you has been sexually assaulted or endured domestic violence. This book undoubtedly exposes this harsh reality, but more importantly offers invaluable insight into what each of us can do to protect ourselves and those around us. Steve Thompson, the founder and owner of No Zebras productions, has made it his life's work to understand the "whys" and "hows" of sexual aggression. His research has consisted of over 40 years of interviewing offenders, law enforcement, psychologists, doctors, and survivors. His unique perspective of sexual and domestic violence brought to light many influencing factors, warning signs, and key elements seen in these crimes. From this research, Thompson developed No Zebras, No Excuses - a program aimed to educate the audience on sexual aggression and bystander behavior.

## What it means to be a zebra

So, you may be wondering what does it mean to be a zebra? Imagine for a moment a herd of zebras. Suddenly, a lion sprints toward the herd. Instinctively, the zebras run. The herd runs as the lion continues his pursuit, but as you might have suspected, the weaker zebras in the back start to lose steam and fall behind. Eventually, the lion pounces on one of the most vulnerable zebras. Pay attention because here is the takeaway: as the lion devours his prey the herd stops and is watching just a short distance away. One zebra is thinking, "Thank God it wasn't me." The zebra next to her thinks, "No wonder she fell prey, she never pays attention." Another zebra in the herd simply looks away from the carnage because it's too hard to think about. No matter the reason, no matter the excuse, a zebra is always a zebra. This analogy explains how bystander behavior works. Neglecting to protect or stand-up for the victim, placing blame on the victim rather than the offender, and pretending not to notice are all bystander behaviors.

## Bystander Effect

Understanding and confronting the bystander effect head on is how we change the culture. Sexual violence and domestic violence have not become epidemics in our culture solely because of offenders. This is an epidemic fueled by two factors. The first is a diffusion of responsibility; a phenomenon that occurs when little to no action is taken within a group, not because no one cares, but because everyone assumes the person next to them will take responsibility. The second factor fueling the epidemic is rape culture. The all too common myths such as "she must have wanted it, look at what she was wearing," and "boys will be boys," contribute to the lack of offenders being held accountable as often as they should. Thus, they have the opportunity to offend again and again. The myth that offenders are easy to spot makes it possible for offenders to hide in plain sight. Our culture has made it unsafe for victims to come forward. Fear of not being believed is their major concern. Too often, the victims' pain, their stories, and their voices are silenced. This is *caused* because a predator chose to inflict pain on someone and is *perpetuated* because individuals who saw or knew it *chose* to do or say nothing.

**My Story**

On a Wednesday night in 2016, my first week of classes junior year of college, I was sexually assaulted. And despite what rape culture may have wanted me to believe, I was NOT raped because I went out for drinks on a Wednesday night. I was NOT raped because I met a boy I hardly knew. I was NOT raped because I consumed alcohol. I was raped because a guy planned to, intended to, and chose to rape me. Simple as that. But for the sake of explaining how my experience relates to No Zebras, No Excuses, I will not focus on the offender; rather, I'll focus on the zebras of my story.

The guy I planned to meet at the bar who we will call Zebra A was not the guy who raped me. He introduced me to the guy who did, who we will label, "offender". Zebra A, unknown to me until I arrived at the bar, brought a woman with him to the bar. We will refer to her as Zebra B. After I had consumed only one beer, I began to feel strange. Witnesses stated I began to talk louder. I remember noticing I had very little motor control, which increasingly became worse. At this time, the offender asked me if I'd like to go to his place, called a cab, and unlike me, I left with him without protest. The cab driver, Zebra C, no doubt noticed me drift in and out of consciousness in the cab. It was also apparent I hardly knew the offender and we were being dropped off at his house. Upon getting out of the cab, I fell on the ground. Zebra C witnessed this happen, yet still chose to drive away. Minutes later I was vomiting, and the offender called Zebras A and B to come over and help him. The offender and Zebra A reported they were drinking whiskey while Zebra B helped clean me up. Zebra B reported I was unable to state where I lived and couldn't provide any phone numbers for her to call.

Once I had passed out, Zebra A and B decided to leave me in the offender's room. They claim the offender told them both he would sleep on the couch. Once they left the house, I was raped.

It is important to mention the offender was the active student government president of the university. Unbeknownst to me, when it became public that the offender had been charged with criminal sexual conduct, the student government decided to take a group vote. They were faced with the decision of either publicly addressing the university about what actions they would take regarding the accusations made against their president or to sweep the matter under the rug. The student government, who I will refer to as Zebra D, decided almost unanimously not to make any statement and sweep the matter under the rug.

Almost a full year after charges were filed, after I had testified in court and a judge found there to be enough probable cause for the case to go to trial, the prosecutor (Zebra E) informed me that all charges were being dropped. The victim advocate (Zebra F) sat in the corner of the room as he said this and chose to say nothing. I learned that the interim head prosecutor (Zebra G), had instructed Zebra E to break this news to me and lie about the reasons why, leaving me even more confused and in the dark. This is how I met Steve Thompson. He was made aware of the lies I had been told and immediately stepped in to tell me the truth. He reached out to Zebra G and made it clear that I did not deserve to be lied to. To have someone stick up for me when so many people remained silent gave me the strength I needed to keep fighting.

My counselor at the time (Zebra H), rather than validating my concern, told me I needed to calm down and let the people that "knew what they were doing" have a chance to explain. Over the following months, while I considered ways in which I could hold the offender accountable for what he did to me, Zebra H believed I had become obsessive and could not let go.

Three years later, after the attorney general's office reinstated the charges that had been previously dropped, I watched as the offender was sentenced to prison and convicted of criminal sexual conduct. When I think back to every battle I was faced with, all the countless moments I felt completely alone, and every moment I felt like I couldn't go on, I still think about these zebras. I think about how I could have endured fewer battles, could have felt like people had my back, and could have felt hopeful if even one of these zebras had made a choice to not be a bystander. Zebras A and B could have made sure I was in a safe place. Zebra C could've called an ambulance. Zebra D could have acted with transparency by informing the university that their president assaulted a student and would not be welcome back. Zebra E and Zebra F could have advocated on my behalf. All they had to do was say something. It was apparent on their faces they knew the decision was unjust, but they stayed silent. Zebra G had a responsibility to allow a jury to decide the fate of the offender, but instead he robbed me of my day in court. Zebra H grew tired of the stress and hopelessness of the situation. She chose to see me as the broken one, rather than the unjust system I was up against.

I found zebras in the student body population. I found them in the transportation system. Even worse, I found them in the mental health and law enforcement professions – professions based on a foundation of protecting the vulnerable. If even one of these zebras had spoken up when it mattered, my situation could have been drastically changed for the better. You may feel like you don't make a big difference, but often times the power of one can make a world's difference. I was drowning in a sea of zebras. It saddens me to think back to how hard I had to fight for justice and the toll it took on me. The injustice I fought wasn't only caused by the rapist but by the zebras who enabled him.

There were times when I felt as if people believed that if someone else is fighting, then their voice doesn't need to be heard. FALSE. One voice can create a ripple, but voices raised in numbers will make waves. I am one person. I made my small dent, but my story is one of thousands that deserve to be heard. I've heard it said how far we've come since Larry Nassar was sentenced, but how far have we truly come when it takes hundreds of survivors' voices to make someone listen? This is a reality I wish was not the case. We are all part of this, whether our lives have been affected by sexual assault or not. We all make a choice every single day. We either stand up and take action, or we choose to do nothing. Bystanders are not just found in bars and house parties. Bystanders are those that understand the problem at hand but cannot see a connection between the victim's story and their own reality. The justification for releasing themselves from responsibility is a choice in itself and is a poor one.

To put it bluntly, bystander behavior is no less guilty than purposely imposing harm to someone. No matter the age, title, experience, or level of authority, no one is excused from witnessing harm done to another and looking the other way. We are all better than that and we all have the choice to rise above. Living out what is easiest and what draws the least attention may be the safer option, but no one remembered in our history ever did what was easy. Those we admire and revere most did what was right, despite the risk it posed and the conflict it would surely spark.

Ellie Weisel, one of my all-time favorite authors as well as a survivor of the Holocaust said, "I swore never to be silent whenever and wherever human beings endure suffering and humiliation. We must always take sides. Neutrality helps the oppressor, never the victim. Silence encourages the tormentor, never the tormented."

The next time you see something that gives you reason to pause or hear something that just doesn't sit right with you, don't be a zebra. Don't assume someone else will help. Be the person that Steve Thompson was to me. The next time you're given the opportunity, show someone they matter. Show someone that you see them, you hear them, and you value them. When we act like zebras, we show people they aren't worth protecting.

Stephen Thompson

# ONE

# SEXUAL AGGRESSION AND YOU

S exual assault, stalking, partner violence and harassment are horrible things to think about. You are probably saying to yourself, "this isn't something I want to read; I don't care about this; it can't affect me." I truly wish this was the case, but the facts dispel this belief. Sexual assault, stalking, partner violence, and harassment affects you, your friends, your family and the strangers you see around you.

My involvement with sexual aggression began as a young black belt instructor teaching at a mid-western university. Several young women in the community had been raped over the course of five months, and I was asked to teach a self-defense class for women. I knew nothing of the issue. I had not read an article, a book nor ever heard the voice of a survivor, yet I was selected as an expert on the topic because I had a black belt. Because by nature I am a bit anal retentive/ compulsive obsessive, I really wanted to do the right thing with my students. I likened sexual assault to a street fight. I knew about street fighting, so I used what I knew and thought I did a good job of teaching and preparing these young women to fight an attacker. Unfortunately, I was terribly wrong. On April 12, of 1973, one of those young women from my class was raped. She said, "I did everything you taught me, why did this happen?" She trusted me to teach her to protect herself and I felt that I had betrayed her.

## THE SILENT CRIMES

Hers was the first survivor's voice I ever heard, and I still hear it in my mind today. Her assault was my failure; a failure to understand the realities of sexual assault. It was that day, and that young woman's voice that drove me to look critically at self-defense strategies; to understand who rapists are and how they go about the process of assaulting innocent boys, girls, men and women.

Sexual assault, stalking, harassment, and partner violence happen everywhere. Schools and communities that say they have no problem are simply ignoring the realities. Perhaps they do this out of ignorance; perhaps they do not want to alarm anyone and perhaps they are concerned about the public relations issues presented by people who perpetrate sexual aggression. Regardless of the rationale, institutions and communities that are truly educated on these topics, put safety, education, and awareness ahead of other concerns.

How big is the problem of sexual aggression? Approximately one in four college women will be the victim or survivor of a completed act of rape and approximately one in 16 men. (1) It is estimated that 15 percent of women and 6 percent of men will be stalked during their lifetime with the college numbers being even higher. (2) One out of every five long-term relationships at college involves some form of abuse. (3) Finally, whether school or work related, it is difficult to find a person that cannot give personal examples of being harassed or bullied. Each of us will be affected by sexual aggression in some way. It may happen to you, a roommate, friend, family member or partner directly.

Regardless of the circumstance, this is about you, your awareness and your desire to make this a safer more respectful community.

With sexual aggression being such a problem why don't we hear about it more? The truth is because we have not created an environment that understands and supports individuals who are the targets of sexual aggression. Most survivors do not report the crime because:

• They feel no one will believe them.

• They feel people will blame them for what happened.

• They make excuses for the offender.

• They blame themselves.

• They are made to feel responsible for the situation.

• They do not identify it as an assault.

We must understand there is a big difference between **responsibility** and **judgment.** Consider these real-life examples. Many years ago, a young woman was blamed for being raped by the then heavyweight boxing champion of the world because she simply went to his room. A second example happened in a small Colorado town after an 18-year-old young woman brought charges against a well know NBA basketball star. Do you think the news coverage and the attitudes of people were neutral or were the young woman's past and present behavior the issue? Not long-ago headlines were made after a New York college student was blamed for being beaten and raped because she chose to jog late at night. A final example is a midwestern college student who survived a brutal assault. She was made to feel responsible because she allowed a man to walk her home after having a drink with him. In all these examples survivors are generally looked at by society as being somewhat or totally responsible for the behavior of the offender.

Think for a moment, if a man is robbed outside of an ATM late at night is his behavior, his dress, the location or time of day the issue? Or is the issue he was robbed? When are we going to hold offenders completely responsible for their behavior? The behavior of a survivor before and during an assault should not be the issue. The focus should be on the fact that they did not give consent. Behavior is a function of the choices we make. When someone rapes through force, coercion, or using alcohol or other drugs to gain control, it is a conscious choice the offender made! When someone makes repeated calls, waits outside class or work, uses social media to contact the person after they were repeatedly told to stop, they are making a choice to stalk! When someone treats their partner in a way, they themselves would not want to be treated, they are making a choice to do so! I have worked with thousands of incidents of sexual aggression. Not once have I seen the target to be responsible. Certainly, there may be instances where judgment could be questioned but never is the target of sexual aggression or the target of any crime for that matter, responsible for the behavior of the offender. No one makes them do it, it is a conscious choice. In fact, most times offenders think about what they are going to do ahead of time. It is time we stop making excuses and blaming survivors for the behavior of others. Behavior is a function of choice!

Certainly, we can think it not sound judgment to drink with someone we hardly know and then go to a location where others are not around. However, if that person is then raped it was the choice of the rapist. The offender is always responsible for their own behavior. No one made the man rape the New York jogger, tease the classmate, beat his wife/girlfriend/partner, or stalk someone. Offenders act out sexually aggressively because they want to. It is all about power, control, and conquest.

## ARE MEN TO BLAME?

The purpose of this book is to address the most common realities of sexual aggression. I am acutely aware that men are assaulted, stalked, harassed, and abused in relationships. I am aware these crimes readily occur in the gay and lesbian communities. I have profiled women who offend. Though the settings may differ, my experience is that the dynamics are basically the same.

The simple fact is, whether the target of sexual aggression is an adult or child, male or female, the clear majority of offenders are male. (4) It is generally men who assault, stalk, harasses, engage in partner violence and assault children and it is about time males step up and say NO MORE!

## WHY IS THIS STILL A PROBLEM TODAY, AND WHY IS IT GENERALLY MEN WHO COMMIT THE CRIMES?

Some say sexual aggression is less of a problem today than a decade ago. Most experts strongly disagree with this because the factors that contribute to some males being aggressive towards others have not changed and in fact have gotten worse. Are women less objectified today than in the past? What about in advertising? Frequently we see females in a variety of different suggestive postures promoting beer, auto parts, etc. When was the last time you saw a man in his boxers in an ad for chain saws? Does the media portray women and men equally or does sex sell? What we have are many young boys who are continually bombarded with images of women as sexual objects, as nothing more than things. For many of these boys their only role models are professional athletes, politicians, and TV or movie actors. Many of these models are truly good, but they do not get the headlines. Bad behavior makes headlines and creates "buzz".

The point is many of us are not seeing females any differently today than a decade ago. She is not a total person but rather she is hair, breasts something to pursue and conquer. Many men today are neither less aggressive nor more respectful towards others. Thus, the problem of sexual aggression continues.

In the early 1980's sexual assault, harassment and dating/domestic violence began to be a topic of interest and discussion. Countless survivors felt their experiences were finally being understood. They would come forward and talk about their experiences. More reported and more endured the court process but unfortunately survivors found little had changed. They were still being held responsible for what happened to them. They still had to provide more proof that a crime had occurred as opposed to victims of other types of crimes such as theft. They still had to confront a culture that did not want to believe that men and boys would do this without being teased and provoked. The problem of confusing judgment with responsibility still reared its ugly head.

As was already mentioned, approximately one in four college age women will be the victims of a sexual assault. This means there are many women walking the sidewalks of universities, colleges, schools and communities who have experienced an assault. Reports, however, are extremely low. More than 9 out of 10 go unreported (5), leaving the survivor frequently feeling isolated from support while the predator goes about life with no consequences. It is our responsibility as administrators, peers, friends and members of this society to create a culture that supports survivors of sexual aggression so they can come forward and be treated the same as survivors of virtually all other crimes. Think about if a hundred people in your community were robbed. How many would report? Most likely, all. Think about the differences between how survivors of robbery are treated versus people who have been sexually assaulted. Knowing this, what do we frequently hear addressed? The false reporting of this crime. The fact is false reporting is no more likely in sexual assault than in other crimes. (6) If there are one hundred people claiming they were raped, approximately five will be lying. (7) The perception, however, is people lie about being raped. There is absolutely no research, no proof that this is true. It is a myth that has been perpetrated for generations. Some of the most emotional voices I hear belong to dads, brothers, husbands, friends and partners of survivors. They are frustrated and angry because they feel the survivor close to them is not being believed or worse, being blamed for what happened. Though I never say it I must admit to wondering sometimes if that survivor was someone else's daughter, son, wife, friend or partner would they blame and doubt, or would they believe and support?

We all have the power to change the culture of survivor blaming. The important idea to keep in mind is our own individual sphere of influence; how are you setting up a safe place for those around you; those you are responsible for and to? The bottom line is sexual aggression affects us all. Every one of us has someone we know who has been, or will be sexually assaulted, stalked, harassed or suffered abuse by a partner. They will likely not tell anyone, but they exist, nonetheless. A harsh reality is the perpetrator is most likely someone known to the survivor. Think about the messages we send our college age young people and children. "Don't walk alone, don't talk to strangers, always lock your door", though sound advice for reducing some risk of being assaulted by a stranger, we rarely stress the real risk; the danger that lies with the person who is a date or acquaintance of the target, the neighbor, a partner or someone we casually know. This will be addressed in later chapters.

### LOOKING AT BYSTANDERS AS A "ZEBRA"

Incidents of sexual aggression rarely happen where others are not aware. The man who assaults someone he knows generally tells others about it. The harasser must have an audience. Individuals who are physically and emotionally abused show signs that other frequently choose to ignore. Zebras represent what many around us do daily. Picture lions hunting; what animal do they frequently find? The innocent zebras! Lions stalk the heard and then attack the weakest, slowest, most vulnerable. The chase is on; a lion gets one zebra out of the herd and quickly brings it down. As the lion feeds on the fallen zebra the rest of the heard will stop a short distance away and watch one of their own being devoured. What are they thinking? I would bet it is something like "glad that wasn't me". Perhaps they distance themselves from the fallen zebra by telling themselves they didn't know that zebra. Regardless, the next day the chase is on and another zebra is killed. With the herd once again looking on thinking, "she should have seen it coming, that will never happen to me or any of my family."

People are the same way as it relates to sexual aggression. Thinking it will never happen to them or anyone they care about. Most men would say they would never rape, harass, stalk or abuse their partners, but what about the party where someone is singled out because they had too much to drink or possibly had alcohol or drugs pushed on them? Men and women see that person being led away, yet no one gets involved. If just one man, one person would stand up and stop it or if their friends would intercede that person would not be victimized. Does anyone step forward? Generally, not. Much like the zebra they stand by and watch. Maybe they make an excuse; maybe they just look the other way. Regardless of what goes through their mind, they do nothing. We have got to eliminate this zebra, myth-based mentality. Accepting violence and aggression against one woman or man is to accept violence against all. When one man acts our sexually aggressively all males must take it personally. It reflects on us all!

Gaining knowledge about this issue will place a responsibility on you. You will notice behaviors that are simply not right; behaviors that can negatively affect someone. You will be put in a position where your interpretation of what you are seeing will force you to decide. Your decision can take one of three paths:

Path One – **Participate** in actions that have a range of negative consequences to other. Actions prompted by:

• Need for attention

•Social norms

• Lack of empathy

• Objectification of the target

• Being a follower and conforming to the group

• Fear of being singled out by not conforming

Path Two – **Ignore** the behavior you are seeing; the "zebra" mentality.

• Feel no obligation to help

• Rationalize inaction

• Feel you are possibly wrong

• Justify the behavior you are seeing

Path Three – **Intercede** by doing something that will stop the behavior.

• Taking safe and positive action to help

• Being a catalyst for action

• Having the courage to act

You can be the individual, the friend, the group that says, "NO MORE'. Gandhi once said, "you have to be the change you want to see." If we want to see people treated equally, fairly with dignity and respect we must get involved. If we want to see a society that does not look at women, girls, gays, lesbians, and trans as objects or somehow less important, we must get involved. If we want to see people stop being spectators, we must get involved. If we want to see an end to victim blaming and an end to sexual aggression on our campus, in our community, and in society, we must get involved. I believe that by reading this book and working to eliminate the zebra mentality you are taking the first step to ending sexual aggression. No more zebras and no more excuses!

### KEY POINTS OF THIS BOOK
• What are the realities of sexual aggression?

• Who are the perpetrators?

• Why do they choose to behave in ways that hurt others?

• What are the laws related to sexual aggression?

• How can we reduce our risk and the risk of others for being targets of sexual aggression?

• And finally, what can we all do to create an environment where sexual aggression is not tolerated. A society where the bystander "Zebra" does not exist.

# *Wake it or Not*

*Hatred. So tangible*

*Feel it. Hard. Cold.*

*Hatred manifested.*

*It watches through eyes as icy as the heart of.*

*It waits. Violence!*

*Serenity returns. Hatred bides it's time until it can happen again.*

*Flame into vengeance and destroy*

*That which woke it from its slumber.*

Anonymous survivor

# TWO

# SEXUAL ASSAULT

*"When you're raped it takes YOU, and YOU won't ever come back. I can't wake up and have it gone and be the person I once was."* Survivor

S exual assault, whether by a stranger or someone the survivor knows can be devastating to an individual and to the community in which it occurs. For colleges located in smaller communities, and smaller communities themselves, stranger assault is a rare occurrence. Urban communities and colleges located within them have higher incidences of stranger assault. However, over eighty percent of the assaults within those urban communities are committed by someone known to the target. (8) For purposes of clarity, to describe an assault or assailant where the two people know each other, the term **Familiar** will be used. Where the two people do not know each other, the term **Stranger** will be used. Though both stranger and familiar assault will be addressed, the greater emphasis will be on sexual assault where the offender is known to the target.

Stephen Thompson

## *DOES THIS REALLY HAPPEN HERE?*
I hear this comment often as I travel throughout the country. Statistics can be used to prove or disprove almost anything. If just one person we know is sexually victimized, it is significant. However, the reality is that half of the women you know will be targeted by a sexual predator; roommates, classmates, friends, and family members. What about the males you may know? They are at risk as well; especially the young men. Of those individuals targeted and confronted by a predator, few will get away. Unfortunately, most will not. This is not an indictment on the choices made by the survivor prior or during the assault, but rather a statement based on the fact that there are many different profiles of sexual predators. The choice to resist may work with one perpetrator such as the "Neighborhood Voyeur", but unfortunately it does not work with the "Retaliator." There is no full-proof method of avoiding a sexual assault. Most people targeted never think it will happen to them; it is always someone else. I have found that those who think it will never happen to them are more at risk than those of us who acknowledge that bad things can happen to good people. It is not about living in fear but rather understanding it can happen and learning what can be done to minimize our risk.

The answer to "Does It Happen Here?" is obviously yes; here and everywhere. Knowing this, why is it that we do not hear about sexual assault more often? The fact is that most sexual assaults are not reported (9). There are several reasons for this. Frequently, survivors do not feel they will be believed. Some feel responsible because they were led to believe that sexual assault is a communication problem and they did not communicate well enough. This is not true but will be dealt with later in this chapter. Some do not report because they believe it cannot be a sexual assault if you know the person or if you engaged in foreplay before saying no.

This self-blame and doubt are a part of our society's belief system based historically on the attitudes of two men. In the late 1600's, a judge in England named Lord Hale was adjudicating a rape case. Hale ruled that the offender was not guilty. In the written brief by Lord Hale, he justified his decision by basically saying it is easy for the "victim" to make a claim of rape but very hard for the offender to defend himself. (10)  This is where the "he said/she said" description of the crime first surfaced;  a description heard often today. This description creates doubt on the validity of the claim by indicating that it is a crime that must have witnesses to be believed.  I would argue that many crimes are without witnesses other than the victim and offender such as burglaries and car theft, yet the victim is generally not doubted to the extent they are in sex crimes.

The second major influence was Sigmund Freud in the 1880's (11).  He believed that women fantasize about being raped and that women say no when they mean yes. It was also his attitude that women are confused about sex and consequently do not make good witnesses in court. I would challenge any reader to produce credible research that validates the statements of Freud. The fact is, the opposite of Freud's belief is true. However, I seriously doubt few reading this could honestly say they have not heard statements or even had thoughts similar to those of Hale and Freud. These two men created a false narrative that today leads many to make assumptions about the crime of sexual assault and its survivors,  resulting in conclusions that are not true. These myth-based attitudes adversely affect how these crimes are treated by the legal system, the media, society in general, and specifically, the people most closely affected.

Creating a supportive, informed community through fact-based information can go a long way in establishing an environment where survivors of sexual assault will be treated with the same dignity and respect as survivors of all other crimes. In order to do accomplish this, you will need to recognize and eradicate the myths surrounding sexual assault and come to understand the realities that you will learn from this book.

## WHAT IS SEXUAL ASSAULT?

Rape, sexual misconduct, sexual assault, forced sodomy, sexual battery and more are words used in a legal sense to describe essentially the same illegal behavior. These terms would seem to indicate different crimes, but the reality is that they all refer to the same violation. I prefer to use only one term, sexual assault. This encompasses oral, anal, vaginal penetration as well as contact (touching) breast, genital, and buttock area. I define sexual assault as: *anytime anyone does anything of a sexual nature where there is not clear, active participatory consent and/or where the target is underage or under the influence of drugs or alcohol.* I did not make excusing statements such as: unless they had sex before; unless she/he had been drinking; unless the offender was teased or led on; or unless "she let things get out of control." Without clear consent, it is never the fault of the target for what was done to them, never!

Several years ago, I was speaking to a Division I football team on this subject. The players asked a variety of questions about consent that indicated to me a level of confusion. To make it clear we discussed words they would associate with Consent, Coercion and Force. I used their words to create a visual that I believe eliminates any confusion and gray areas.

| CONSENT | COERCION | FORCE |
|---------|----------|-------|
| We/Us | I/Me | Intimidate |
| Mutual | Pressure | Threaten |
| Welcomed | Deceit | Violence |

One of the players looked at this and shouted, "I get it! The rule is simple; left is right, and right is wrong!" I thought about it, laughed with the team but acknowledged that the rule is very simple. Anytime you move to the right towards Coercion you are in the wrong. This takes any assumptions out of it. Anything to the right of Consent is wrong, no excuses. Most people expect Force will be used during an assault. Though this is rarely the case, it is the expectation in society. We need to remember that the behavior of the survivor is not the question or the issue; it is the behavior of the offender. However, when it comes to Coercion the line between legal and illegal, right and wrong seems to blur for many. I believe the reason for this is that they cannot grasp the basic fact that sexual assault is a planned act. It is not an impulse caused by the survivor or alcohol. The fact that there are men who want to do this and actually plan to do it, is somehow difficult for many people to understand. It is far easier to place the blame for the offender's behavior on something the survivor did to bring it on. Unfortunately, survivors sometimes do this as well to rationalize a situation they emotionally are not ready to cope with. So, instead of seeing the assault for what it is, the survivor frantically searches for details they missed, actions they could have taken, actions they should have refrained from, etc. The brain wants an answer that makes sense. And simply put: It is very difficult for a good person to truly grasp another person's intent to do harm.

The next part is perhaps the most important information contained in this book. Read on and reflect on some of your own attitudes.

## FAMILIAR ASSAULT

The term date/acquaintance rape has been used for many years to describe the relationship between offender and survivor. Unfortunately, this term has had a profoundly negative impact on survivors. There are reasons for this. In a study I conducted in the mid 90's, my research partner and I created a survey that asked twelve simple questions relating to three scenarios; a date rape, an acquaintance rape, and stranger rape. The results were predictable, yet it gave concrete evidence showing the more a scenario indicated familiarity between the offender and survivor, the more responsibility was given to the survivor. When people heard or read the word "date," the survivor was held more responsible than when the word "acquaintance" was used. The survivor was held least often responsible when "stranger" was indicated. When alcohol was present in the "date" or "acquaintance" scenario, the blame was given even more to the survivor. These results showed that victim blaming increases as university students, community members, and people within the legal system perceived, through the words date, acquaintance, that the two people knew each other.

I have heard many statements such as: "Wonder what she/he did to cause this?" "He/she should have known better than to go to his place." "They drank together." "He is such a nice, good looking guy." "She/he led him on the whole night." Not only have I heard these statements, but survivors hear them as well. When assault survivors hear statements such as these, it affects them by generally increasing the level of responsibility and blame they place upon themselves. Is it any wonder why the report rate for this type of assault is so low?

There are many misconceptions when it comes to a sexual assault where the survivor knows the assailant. Foremost among them is this one: is the survivor responsible in some way? If the survivor went to the offender's room, consumed drinks purchased for them, or if they had sex together on a previous occasion, these behaviors imply consent in the minds of many. Another major misconception is that familiar rape is not as traumatic when compared to stranger rapes. Consequently, many believe it should not merit the attention and concern of stranger rape. This could not be further from the truth; quite the opposite. The betrayal by someone you thought you knew and trusted is an added source of trauma in familiar rape.

A woman I spoke with a few years ago at a training told me of her assault and the terrible aftermath. She had been working at a local convenience store in her small town with two young men that she went to high school with. They worked together for several nights when one night she was in the stock room getting some cereal for the shelves and one of the boys came in. They spoke for a few minutes when he asked her to perform oral sex on him. She laughed thinking he was joking. He became angry and grabbed her hair. When she yelled for help the other worker came to see what was happening. Instead of stopping the assault he laughed and said it was something he has been wanting to do. They took turns assaulting her, laughing and calling her names the entire time. When they were finished assaulting her, they told her she was a slut and wanted it. She left, never telling anyone until we spoke a few years after the assault. When we spoke, it was like the incident just happened. She cried and was hardly able to complete a sentence while telling me she hasn't been out with a man since; hasn't been able to go into any convenience store since, and when she sees that breakfast cereal, she gets sick.

A young man I know was assaulted by his middle school teacher. Still today he looks skeptically at any man who is a teacher. There are voices of survivors like these all around us if only we could make them comfortable enough to speak so we could listen and believe. The trauma survivors experience before, during and after an assault cannot and should not be judged by others. It is very real and very personal. I have listened to the voices of thousands of survivors during my career and can say unequivocally the psychological aftermath to familiar assault is equal to and frequently greater when the offender is known. In addition to the trauma frequently experienced by most survivors of sexual assault, such as the loss of control, feelings of vulnerability and self-blame; one who is assaulted by someone they know often feels betrayed. They question their ability to judge people. A college student I spoke with indicated she wants to get married some day and have children; yet, she can't date because she trusted once and was raped. Every day she questions herself, her future. Her pain and sense of loss is palpable, even to someone who has never had such an experience.

## WHO IS THE FAMILIAR OFFENDER, AND HOW DOES HE ASSAULT?

Many years ago, when I was a college athlete my coaches taught me I needed to know my opponent and their techniques to best find a way to defeat them. Obviously sexual aggression is not a game; however, by knowing how these men do it, and who they are, one can better understand what it takes to reduce risk. If you remember, I got into this field after I was asked to teach self-defense to women. I believed I did a good job with the class even though I had never read a book, research article, or even spoke with a survivor. I was the black belt expert. After one of my students was raped, I read every book and article I could find on the issue. I needed to know more. A realization soon came to me that no one was talking with offenders. The more you know about your opponent... How could I be effective in this field if I didn't know him? So, I asked our local sheriff if I could speak with jailed sex offenders. He agreed and that was the start of my real education. I moved from local jails to our state prison system. Within two years I applied to take a leave from teaching (sabbatical) to visit prisons throughout the country getting the who, how and why of rape. For example, most self-defense classes offered to women today spend a great deal of class time learning to get away from attacks from the rear. I found the reality is that offenders rarely attack from behind. Why? Because they gain psychosexual gratification by looking into the eyes of the target. They like to see the shock and fear they have suddenly created. It gives them a sense of power. A secondary reason is they mostly approach the target from the front, face to face, because they like to get physically close before the attack. They may ask simple questions to the victim such as the time, or directions. They may pose as someone such as a new neighbor, utility worker, or someone in need of medical assistance, all the while moving closer and closer. I learned much from offenders and realized most individuals that give advice about sexual aggression know little of the true realities of sexual assault.

In the following pages you will learn about the process and the personalities involved with both stranger and familiar rape.

### "NICE GUYS" RAPE

"He was such a nice guy, we talked, and I thought I could trust him because he was so nice to me." In speaking with literally thousands of survivors, their initial description and perception is just that quote. The perception initially was that their assailant was a very nice guy. Because of this often-repeated statement, the label **"Nice Guy"** will be used to describe him. Please understand there is a huge difference between good men and "Nice Guys". Good is a quality that runs to the heart of most men. It involves respect for themselves, their character and their integrity. Predators use the nice guise as a tactic or strategy to gain the trust of their intended target. He is a very perceptive chameleon who can read his intended target's body language and words. This chameleon shows his true colors to men who are close to him, but to his intended targets he will be whatever he thinks they need to see to gain their trust.

Through my early years of research and continued involvement with survivors, predators and investigations, the basic predator profile I published in 1995 is even more accurate today (12). His basic profile embodies several of the following characteristics:

• He is an athletic, body-conscious male. In high school, he was/is probably an athlete involved in a team sport.

• He cannot pass his image in a mirror or window without looking at himself. His two most favorite words are I/Me. Everything must revolve around him. He is outwardly confident but is generally insecure. Truly confident people do not have to prove themselves to anyone. They do not need to be the center of attention. The "Nice Guy" does.

• He is attractive, personable and well-liked by people of both genders. He generally has little trouble attracting potential targets.

• He needs to be around men in groups. For example: fraternities, sport clubs or teams, civic groups. He will go to bars frequently with his friends. It does not mean all men who are involved in these groups are potential predators. It means that this man gravitates towards groups where he can be around men.

• He does not generally engage in long-term committed relationships. He dates many different people but does not commit to one.

• He is egocentric and self-serving where he needs to guide conversations and situations so that he is the center of attention.

• This "Nice Guy" brags to his friends about his sexual conquests, real or fabricated.

• He does not handle rejection or criticism well. This is evidenced by his need to be liked by those around him. He will generally be the dominant male in a group, surrounding himself with followers who will support him.

• He believes potential targets are simply objects, and he has the right to aggressively take from them what he wants. His attitude is that he is superior, and they are inferior to him.

• He is rarely patient enough to groom his intended target through multiple dates or encounters. He will either "score" (coerce), use force to get what he wants (no consent) or give up with this contact by the third time he is in a situation where he can isolate his target.

• If he gets what he wants but his target later involves law enforcement, he may eventually admit to using coercion involving alcohol as a tool to gain control or possibly force if the coercion fails. However, he will **ALWAYS** say she was responsible for what happened by stating she led him on, she wanted it, etc. He does not see this as rape. His goal is the sexual conquest, even if he needs to use force to get it. It is likely he would pass a polygraph if asked "did you rape?"

• Due to the nature of his personality, the "Nice Guy" is rarely seen as a self-serving predator. You can't identify him by his grades, his looks, or basic personality. People who know him would think him incapable of an assault. People who do not know him would see a "Nice Guy" wrongly accused. Generally speaking, the public will side with him and hold his target responsible for either falsely accusing him or implying consent by behaving in such a way as to create confusion on his part.

A popular attitude with familiar assault is that it is a "communication issue" because the target is perceived to inadequately communicate what they wanted or did not want. It is difficult for many to accept that date rape is a planned act. It is much easier to assume some joint responsibility by calling date rape a "grey" area. Is a robbery "grey" if the target is drunk, or wearing expensive clothes while walking alone in a high-risk area? Why is this "grey" term used with sexual assault? I strongly believe it is used because many people find it difficult to accept that men rape because they want to. Holding the target wholly or partly responsible for the rape helps to justify it to those who deny that "Nice Guys" do rape. For example, by believing that the rapist is attracted to certain behaviors of a target such as provocative dress, alcohol use, and risk taking, the deniers do not have to confront the possibility that someone like themselves could be a target. They may tell themselves: "He won't prey on me because I don't display those behaviors." This gives a false sense of safety to people who believe sexual assault is a communication or "grey" issue.

Good men do not make assumptions when it comes to sexual encounters; they stop and clarify. Good men respect themselves. Good men do not use force or pressure. Can you imagine? What does it say about oneself if they feel it is ok to have sex with someone if that person is scared, asleep, forced, pressured, or so drunk they can hardly see him? Good men don't rape or pressure, but "Nice Guys" do.

## HOW DOES THE "NICE GUY" CARRY OUT HIS PLAN?

Virtually every time the "Nice Guy" assaults someone, he follows the same pattern of behavior to accomplish his goal. He is extremely consistent, yet this consistency is at a subconscious level. His behavior involves seven stages with each one being clearly identifiable and building upon the success of the preceding stage. When evaluating avoidance strategies, the strategy must revolve around knowing what he is trying to do – awareness. This can help you avoid a potential problem whether it involves you or someone you know. The term used for the pattern of assault by the "Nice Guy" is the:

## FAMILIAR PREDATOR - SEXUAL ASSAULT SEQUENCE

Step 1: - *Selection of a Target*
This is the most critical stage. If you are not seen as vulnerable, he will not proceed with you but rather find someone else he believes he can successfully target. He is looking for someone whom he knows. Someone he feels will be flattered by his attention. Physical appearance has very little to do with being selected. He may be a friend of a friend, co-worker, someone you have talked with before in a bar or other setting. He prefers targets generally younger. Examples would be:

• In college, he is a junior or senior, targeting a freshman or sophomore at a social setting where alcohol is present.

• In high school, he is the upperclassman taking a freshman to prom.

• He is the sixteen-year-old who just started to drive, cruising into the middle school to find someone who will be flattered by his attention.

• He might be a fifth-year teacher buying drinks for the first-year teacher at the staff after hours bar.

• He could be the veteran sales rep/boss/manager who targets a new employee.

The point to be taken from this is that he is generally the older, more experienced guy in an environment where the target is with friends and feels comfortable. Some of these "Nice Guys" will watch a group of potential targets looking for the one who seems to have consumed the most alcohol. Others are more comfortable planning the specific person to target ahead of time. It is important to understand the "Nice Guy" is a predatory hunter. As he plans his conquest, he will have carefully thought about who, where, and how he will "score."

Step 2: - *Approach and Evaluation*
Once he has chosen his target, he will try to determine if he can get that person to trust him enough to eventually separate them from the people he/she came with. He moves in close, talking very flatteringly the whole time. He will be such a "Nice Guy", offering to get her/him something to drink while continuing his guise of being personable and attentive. Remember, this nice persona is a tactic he uses to gain the trust and control of his target. He is trying to determine if she/he is flattered and responding to him, or if he must try harder. For example; he would approach and ask if he can sit and talk with them while already pulling up a chair. This gives his target little chance to say no. In contrast, a good man would generally allow the person to reject or accept. "Nice Guys' are men who have a difficult time handling rejection. In an environment where alcohol is available, he will be sure to keep a drink in front of his intended target.

"Nice Guys" most often use alcohol and drugs as tools to gain control over their targets while in this second stage. It makes it much easier for them to manipulate their target into leaving with them later. Their preferred drugs can be broken down into four categories:

• First is alcohol. It is the most common, most popular, and socially acceptable tool to obtain and use. At parties, it is very common for him to push fruity flavored, sugar-based drinks that have an extremely high alcohol content. They are cold and taste great with a very powerful result. Another tactic involving alcohol is to "double shot" his target. This means, regardless of the target's favorite drink, he will get them one that has two or more shots. Two drinks like this could be like four or more of what the target would normally drink. He may also push shots as well, using a variety of excuses for the target to drink them.

• Second is gamma hydroxyl butyrate, GHB. This tool is very popular because the predator can make it himself from simple ingredients purchased at any number of large retail stores. When consumed, it makes women extremely uninhibited and sexual. It causes impaired memory and is not detectable in urine after twelve hours. Though it is quite strong tasting and smelling by itself, it can be easily covered in citrus-based drinks. The effects will be felt and observed in five to twenty minutes to such an extent the target dosed will appear extremely drunk.

• Third category are drugs such as rohypnol (roofies), Benadryl, and a variety of others designed to cause relaxation and sleep. Many of these drugs can be purchased legally, but most are purchased illegally or taken from someone's medicine cabinet. Once dosed, the target will become quite sleepy, disoriented, and barely able to function. It is almost impossible to detect in any drink because they do not produce a noticeable odor or taste.

• The final category are the groups of drugs that cause hallucinations. Ecstasy and LSD are the most popular. Often, they are taken willingly, but at times drinks are spiked with them to gain control. When someone is "tripping" they are not in control of themselves nor do they make good witnesses. I worked a case at a western university where young women were given a soft drink where a dot of LSD was placed in the straw. Once the dosed woman started hallucinating, several young men would gang rape the target.

It is extremely important to understand the significance of alcohol and drugs in his sequence of behavior. He uses them as tools to gain trust and control. He needs this trust as he is grooming his target to be submissive to him. These men show a remarkable ability to evaluate a potential target. If he does not get the feeling that he will be successful with this intended target, he will quickly move on to another potential target. However, if he finds he is in control, he will move on to the next stage of the assault pattern.

Step 3: – *Separation*
This stage is critical to his success. If he cannot get his intended target away from supportive people, his rape sequence is stopped. During this stage, he is gathering information critical to the success of his intended assault. Does this target live alone? Are there roommates to deal with? Are there friends of the target who are likely to be concerned? Is the target attentive to him and likely to trust him? By the time he has progressed to this stage, he is relatively sure that when he attempts to get the target to a location where there would be no one to help, the target will be willing to leave with him. Typically, he will use lines such as; "it is too noisy, too smoky, I want to be alone with you, lets watch a movie", etc., etc. He is very charming and manipulative through this stage. It is a game he is playing with the goal of gaining control and trust through his guise of being a nice guy. Here is an example of the "Nice Guy".

*Jenny, a student at a mid-western university, told me this account of her assault. "I went to the bar with several of my friends. We were sitting around talking and having a good time then this guy I sort of new came up and sat down next to me. He was really nice and good looking. He bought me drinks and we talked for a long time. Later I felt him resting his hand on my thigh, but I really didn't think too much about it. At about 11:00 my friends wanted to leave. Jeff told them he would take me home. In a while we left. Jeff asked me if I wanted a cup of coffee before he took me home. Though I don't drink coffee I wanted to spend more time with him, so I said yes. As we passed the restaurant, I asked him where we were going. He told me he likes a special kind of coffee that he has at his place. I became a bit uncomfortable and he must have sensed it because he said, "What's the matter? Don't you trust me?" I felt foolish and apologized. We went to his place and then...How could this have happened to me?"*

By understanding his goal at this stage and monitoring what you and others are drinking, and looking out for one another, the chances of him getting anyone away from the group are very slim. A point to remember is that it is almost always the "Nice Guy" that is the helpful one to the rescue. He is the one who is the first to offer the ride or walk home after spending time with the target.

### Step 4: – *Pressured/Coerced Sex*
Once this "Nice Guy" gets his target to a location where he is comfortable and his target is isolated from any support, he will move quickly to get what he wants. If the target consents and is not coerced through the influence of alcohol, drugs or pressure, the conquest ends. The sex will generally be mutually gratifying though he tends to be self-centered. He will maintain his nice personality and see that she/he gets home. Generally, he tells the target he will call or see them again soon, but rarely does this occur. This was a score, a conquest and he almost never revisits past scores.

When good men are with someone that they want to get intimate with and their partner does not willingly consent, good men will stop and clarify because they respect themselves. However, with "Nice Guys", if the target does not willingly consent, he will keep pushing and pressuring his target into gratifying him. Statements such as: "you owe me; you teased me and you've got me so turned on we have to do this," are all comments that are frequently heard. His goal is to make his target feel responsible for him being sexually excited. If he succeeds in getting her to engage in the behavior he wants, this is coercion not consent. Though it is not right, it is not against the law. If there is no successful coercion or consent, he will cross the legal line and move to the next stage.

Step 5: - *Intimidation*

The goal now is simple, to get what he wants any way he can. Through words and physical force such as holding the target down, removing clothes, immobilizing the hands, forcing the head down, etc., he will let his target know there is no way they will leave until he gets what he wants. Often you will see defense lawyers paint the picture of consent because there is rarely bruising or wounds. Many people who have never been confronted by this kind of aggression believe they would fight, and thus question the behavior of the survivor. Fear, disbelief, confusion, and possibly self-blame are but a few of the reasons the majority of survivors become immobile and do not physically resist. There is a great deal of research explaining this counterintuitive behavior (13). Unfortunately, most within the legal system and our society in general, are unaware of this and continue to question survivor behavior. The important point to consider is the context. Did he tell the target or indicate in any way that they would not be able to leave until he is satisfied? Did the target question their safety if they did not comply? Though rare, there are times when the target will resist, feeling this "Nice Guy" will surely stop. If there is resistance, he will either ignore it and continue or escalate his aggression. He is much different now and no longer the attractive, attentive, nice person but rather a predator focused only on his own gratification. He has the power, the control, and the will to do whatever it takes to get what he wants.

*Amanda was a freshman attending a small college in the east. One night while socializing with her new roommates, the "Nice Guy" she recognized came up to her and started a conversation. She was really flattered because he was popular and one of the older residents. Later, he asked her to come back to his room to watch movies with some of his friends. She agreed and left her friends to go to his room. Once there, he offered her something to drink. They sat on the sofa drinking while waiting for the other people. He began kissing her. Initially she thought it was nice. She soon became concerned because he was trying to put his hands up her shirt. She asked about the others and he said they probably had something else to do. As he became more insistent, she moved his hand and tried to stand up. He would not let her up. She pushed at him and yelled, but he overpowered her. She felt there was nothing she could have done that would have stopped him.*

Step 6:  – *Sexual Violation*

Once he has successfully traumatized his target where she is unable to move or defend herself, and forced to submit to his demands, he is ready to take whatever he wants. He is aggressive, self-centered and in control. Depending on the location and amount of time he has, he could be very quick with his sexual violation, or very creative and slow. If the aggression escalates, so does his tendency to force the target into more degrading acts. Objectification of his target and power over her take on a greater role in his behavior. There are no rules. He has won and will do whatever he wants with this "object".

### Step 7: – *Termination*

After the "Nice Guy" has sexually violated his target, he will either leave, or take his target home. He may act as if nothing is wrong. He could revert to his "Nice Guy" image even saying he had a good time and will call. Others, however, will terminate by taking measures designed to keep the target from telling anyone. He may attempt to make them feel responsible for what has happened by blaming them because of their behavior, dress, reputation, or alcohol consumption. Some will threaten physical retaliation if they tell anyone. Other "Nice Guys" will threaten to tell everyone the target was a slut, someone who "wanted it." He is very convincing. Frequently, the target is confused and disoriented due to alcohol/drugs or shock. They cannot process what has happened to them. Guilt, denial, and societal beliefs make it very difficult for them to hold the "Nice Guy" responsible. Frequently due to ignorance and a myth -based belief system, those close to the target often do not believe them or they minimize what has happened to them. Because of this combination, it is extremely rare for targets to report the assault.

This sequence of rape is extremely consistent to the "Nice Guy." It is important that he finds success with each stage before he proceeds to the next. Failure at one ends the potential assault.

To summarize the behavior sequence of the "Nice Guy":

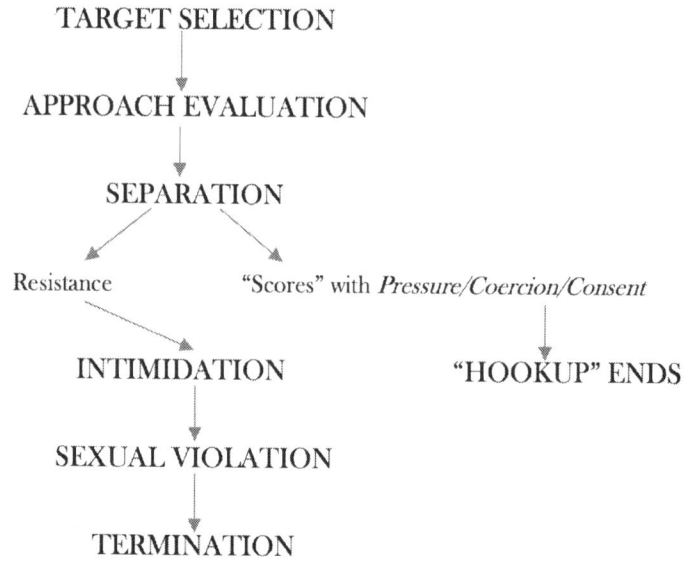

TARGET SELECTION

APPROACH EVALUATION

SEPARATION

Resistance          "Scores" with *Pressure/Coercion/Consent*

INTIMIDATION          "HOOKUP" ENDS

SEXUAL VIOLATION

TERMINATION

## NOW THAT YOU KNOW WHO HE IS AND HOW HE ASSAULTS, WHAT CAN BE DONE TO REDUCE RISK?

Avoiding familiar types of assault starts first with acknowledging that it can happen to you and people you may know. It is not easy to admit this and somewhat scary, however it is a critical step if you want to prevent it. The next step is to become very familiar with the characteristics and behavior of the "Nice Guy". The final step is to consider following the advice based on thousands of people who have talked with me on this subject:

• Believe it can happen to you. The reality is the more we acknowledge the potential for being targeted, the less actual chance it will happen. With this understanding, you will take steps to reduce the chance.

• When attending parties, bars, and other social events, establish with friends that no one is separated or left behind. So often I hear survivors say they were at a bar or party and were left by friends only to have the "Nice Guy" offer help. In other words, look out for each other. Do not allow anyone to be separated from the group, no matter how nice the guy or how good the excuse!

• Do not be afraid to confront behavior that makes you uncomfortable. A touch, comment, or pressure to drink causing the little voice in your head to tell you something doesn't feel right should never be ignored. Ignoring the voice is something very consistent with people who are later assaulted. TRUST THIS VOICE, TRUST YOUR GUT!

• Understand the difference between being alone with someone and being isolated. You can be alone in a room in your apartment but have roommates or friends in the next room in case something goes terribly wrong. Isolation equates to no help and support. Give real thought to not allowing yourself to be isolated with someone until you really feel they can be trusted. Good men are not offended by this because they understand that there are "Nice Guys" out there.

• Ask men you know and trust about the reputation of the man you may be interested in. Men who know him generally see the true person who disrespects potential targets and sees them as simply something to use and discard. Remember, the "Nice Guy" is a chameleon that changes so as to more easily manipulate people.

• Knowing we do not always make good decisions when under the influence of alcohol or drugs, be sure your friends are not Zebras who will let you get separated from them. Work this out ahead of need.

• Always trust your instincts! The first voice in your head expressing concern should override any other voice telling you he is "such a nice guy."

## ZEBRAS AND "NICE GUYS"

It is extremely rare for a "Nice Guy" to operate in an environment where no one can help; where no one notices what is happening. The majority of times when he targets, his target is with friends and he is around men where he has bragged about his intentions. Others will be there to notice his behavior and hopefully interpret it as bad. If you hear a guy talking about getting someone drunk or targeting someone already under the influence, have the courage to do the right thing and get involved. It takes much more courage to stand up for what is right than to go along and be silent. Spill the drink, talk with the target's friends, distract the "Nice Guy" by getting him a drink and separating him from the target, involve other men. There is always something that can be done. For men, the behavior of one man reflects on all men. Saying something like, "come on man, what if you do what you want, and that person tells friends or even the cops. You could lose your job, career and worse. Let's get out of here." I have been contacted by athletes, college men, and military personnel who have used a statement like this successfully to do the right thing. We can either make the decision to stand up and do something positive or stand by and be the do-nothing Zebra. We would all want someone to do the right thing if it was us or someone we care for.

## STRANGER ASSAULT

Sexual assaults by men unknown to the target are rare. As previously mentioned, over 85% of assaults are perpetrated by Familiars with the percentage being higher in more rural settings. Though rare, Stranger assaults are not so rare that we should not address them. University settings can be attractive target zones for Stranger rapists because of the high number of potential targets in a relatively small area. Targets feeling safe because of their environment and a certain amount of naiveté. Strangers have a belief they are smarter than campus security and police in general. On many campus' students live off-campus in apartments or houses within walking distance of their classes. Because of the prevalence of night classes and activities, many people find themselves walking back to their residence during times when few people are present. Some commute to campus via mass transportation or personal vehicles. They find themselves to be frequently alone in parking lots or at public transportation stops. Now that we have established there are opportunities for sexual predators who are the most common Strangers, and what can we do about it?

## WHO IS THE STRANGER, AND HOW DOES HE ASSAULT?

The most likely location of Stranger targeting is in the place you feel the most comfortable; your residence or extension of such as a hotel or office. This particular type of Stranger will be 18-25 years of age. There would be no initial indication of his intention other than perhaps the voice in your head that is uneasy. He may be confident enough to carry on a conversation with you by asking simple directions, time of day, or other small talk. He needs to determine control while getting very close. The most important point is that he will not approach the intended target if there are people around or if he feels you will not be so easily controlled.

The reality is that our place of residence and work are the most likely location for Stranger assault, however, public perception is that "stranger danger" is greatest when we are alone on the street. Though not as common, let's talk about targeting when alone on the street before we address the more frequently seen targeting while inside your residence.

## The "Street"

The street would be defined as anytime you are between two places such as a building and your residence, your car and apartment, etc. The Stranger selects his target based on his perception of risk to himself and the likelihood of success. He most often targets at night in a location he knows and is comfortable with. There will be few witnesses. He selects a target that is alone and appears to him to be vulnerable. I did a study in the early 1990's that included interviewing rapists in prison. Rapists defined a vulnerable victim as one who is alone and appears to be approachable. I learned that size, dress, and beauty have little to do with being selected as a target. Selection boils down to the rapist's perception of the target's vulnerability coupled with a lack of witnesses. He will approach the target from the front or side and attempt to engage them in a brief conversation intended to allow him to get close. Once he is within arm's reach, and after he has determined the target will submit to him, he escalates. He will make it clear what he wants and threatens them if they resist. Because they are alone, afraid and feeling helpless, targets will generally do whatever it takes to survive. This means submitting to his demands. Generally, his intention is to control and have power over his target, but not to beat and physically abuse them. Once he has sexually violated his target, he will leave by either threatening to find them if they call the police, or simply leave with no threat.

Reducing risk with this "Stranger on the Street" starts with acknowledging it can happen. I am not saying that we should live in fear, but rather I am saying we should have a healthy respect for the possibility that this could happen to you and to take steps to reduce the chance. The best advice I can give you is it is easier to avoid this type of assault than to get away once targeted. What I have done myself for decades is acknowledge that though I have the right to be alone on the street, predators could not care less about my rights. Consider doing as I do, look at the times in your daily activities where you are alone and vulnerable. Are there some easy steps you can take to reduce those times of vulnerability? For example; if you work at night or have a night class, can you go to class or work with others? If you drive, can you walk out to your car when others are present? Remember, he looks for targets in situations where there are no witnesses. There are times we all find ourselves alone in potentially vulnerable environments where someone could approach us. What can we do to avoid, or lessen the opportunity for assault?

• Trust your instincts!! If you are walking to your car and something or someone makes you feel uncomfortable, go back inside and/or seek people and shelter. My first martial arts instructor firmly believed that people with bad intentions give off bad energy. I am not sure if it is bad energy or if our minds are such incredible microprocessors that we take in a variety of subtle cues that make us uncomfortable. Regardless, trust the feelings you have and try to get around people. For example, if you are going to your car at an airport or business parking lot and your voice alerts you to a potential situation, turn around and get back to the terminal or business.

• If you find yourself in a situation where you are alone, attempt to create the image of one who is confident and not easily controlled. You are probably saying to yourself, "how do I do that?" In speaking with convicted rapists, I found that they will typically avoid a target that appears to be confident and patiently hunt for a better target. What I repeatedly found was that there were three behaviors we could display that would indicate confidence. First, walk with your head up and make brief eye contact if you see him. Second, take longer steps than you normally would. Third, increase the speed of your walk. Why does this work? Predators are like anyone else; they want to succeed with little effort. If you are creating the illusion of self-assurance they will generally wait until someone else comes along that appears more submissive. It is about success through control and power. Predators believe a confident appearing target is likely to resist and report. This creates a variable they cannot control. Ask yourself this: why would a predator target someone that they perceive would create problems for them when they could fantasize about the next target that would be easy? They are hunters and if hunters fail with the first target, they are anticipating the next. This in itself can be gratifying to them.

• If a man is attempting to speak to you in an environment where you are alone, give a brief answer and close down the conversation while continuing to walk. For example; you are walking from office to car when a man asks for the time. Your response would be to say; " its..., have a nice night." Do not slow and do not make apologies for not stopping. You are assertive yet not aggressive to the point he must respond. If he speaks again, same thing. A brief abrupt answer followed with a statement that indicates you are not stopping to talk. Do not stop as this shows control and lets him into your space.

• If the man blocks your path or physically stops you from leaving, though quite rare, if you appear assertive and continue to create space some will back down when confronted.

• Few strangers will target and escalate with someone who appears self-assured; however, some may escalate verbally and physically to intimidate and gain control. If you are unable to create space because of his actions, you now have the legal right to take whatever action you choose.

• Be aware that aggression calls for an aggressive response. Sometimes it works and sometimes it does not. Take whatever action feels right to you. For some, submission due to beliefs or fear is right. For others, their choice is made by the body's neurobiological response to threat by becoming immobilized. Others may have the ability and aggression to fight. Resistance options can range from screaming and running to physically hurting him by kicking and striking techniques. There is no right or wrong response. Whatever a survivor does or does not do should be completely supported. NEVER is one responsible for being targeted. Behavior is a function of choice and predators are completely responsible for what they do.

Ultimately it is easier to avoid a problem than to get out of it once it starts. Look at the times you are on the street and try to reduce the times you are vulnerable.

### Residence/Indoor Locations

The most likely place for a stranger to target us is in our residence. The place we should feel the most secure is the most frequent site for stranger assault. Do you live by yourself? When are you alone? Do you live in a house or a ground floor apartment? What can you do to minimize risk? There are four basic ways a predator gains access to us when we are in our residence or hotel room. The first way is to simply come through an unlocked door or window. The second is to break in. The third is to do what I call the "Blow Through;" when the door is opened the predator slams through the opening. Put yourself in the mind of the predator while thinking about these previous three methods. What is necessary to know before gaining entry? The answer is, are you alone? It is not realistic that he would come into the residence if you raise Pit Bulls or have the Chicago Bears over for a party. Are you alone!? How does he know? By looking through the windows. Predators rarely put themselves in situations where they can't quickly control the variables. Dogs and multiple people present too many variables for the predator to quickly control. He selects potential targets by watching them to determine vulnerability. The fourth and final way predators gain access is to pose as someone that may have a reason to be at your residence: a repair person for an apartment complex; a delivery person for UPS, Fed Ex., a local flower shop. Perhaps he may pose as someone in sales or someone collecting for a charity. Risk reduction for the four methods/strategies predators use to access targets indoors is relatively simple:

• Where there is an option, live in a third floor or higher apartment that is in a security building requiring keyed access to the main hallway. Third floor or higher makes it next to impossible to look through windows to determine vulnerability. Is there roof access to your floor and building through another building? Security buildings make it much more difficult for a predator to access apartments.

• Whether house or apartment, where possible keep doors and windows as secure as possible. Install security system; cameras; motion detector lights....

• Predators are very aware that most of us are uncomfortable if we are assertive or perceived to be rude. Because of this, the most common way for them to get into our residence or hotel room is to pose as someone that would require your opening the door to them. My general rule is to NEVER open the door, or let anyone into my residence/ hotel room unless:

1. I know and trust them. An example would be if it is my usual maintenance person whom I know well.

2. I am expecting them. Perhaps the local cable company sent a notice indicating repair people would be coming to my place on a specific day.

3. I can call their employer and verify they are who they say.

It is uncomfortable to talk through a closed or chained door because it shows that lack of trust I mentioned, however, it is always easier to keep someone out than to get them out once they are in. By locking doors and not allowing anyone past your door unless they have met the criteria, you have greatly reduced your chances of ever being targeted by a stranger. Review security options for the latest technology....

### THE AFTERMATH

What do I say? How should I act? These are two common questions I am asked by friends, partners, and relatives of sexual assault survivors. It is extremely important to understand survivors are experiencing a variety of emotions. Loss of control, disbelief, shock, guilt, detachment, blame, and fear are but a few. They are forced to reexamine their belief system. Bad things are not supposed to happen to good people. If something like this can happen, what else can happen to them? Can you even imagine how insecure and vulnerable that would make a person feel?

Survivors experience a loss of control. Sometimes they cannot remember exactly what happened due to the effects of drugs, alcohol and their own neurobiological response to trauma. Confusion and vulnerability are words frequently associated with the psychological aftermath of the assault. Once they are safely away from the predator, they may reach out to someone significant for help. Either out of ignorance, anger, frustration or helplessness, that person may react in ways that can cause a survivor to feel challenged and guilty. Never doubt or second-guess the behavior of a survivor. I am frequently called upon as an expert witness to explain the behavior of survivors. "Why didn't they fight? Why no injuries?" These are two frequently asked questions by those close to the survivor as well as people in the legal and medical fields. Generally, people have this clear idea of what a reasonable person would do in that situation, what they in fact would do. Many say they would "fight before they would let that happen." Really? People convince themselves that when confronted by someone generally bigger, stronger, and more experienced with aggression they, their child, partner, or friend would fight? The fact is that most of us, when confronted by aggression, will do whatever it takes to survive. Sometimes our bodies involuntarily make the choice to promote our survival by being unable to move or react. Sexual assault survivors initially experience a phase of trauma called *Impact.* This starts as soon as the offender has used words or physical actions that indicate his intentions. This is when the predator has moved from the stage of Approach/Evaluate to Intimidation. Most survivors I speak with indicate they feel helpless, fear, shock, and disbelief, which results in the strong desire to get through it any way they can. In most cases, this translates into the survivor submitting. They either feel resistance will bring on more violence or their body involuntarily will not let them resist even if they could. The fact is that most people, male or female, are not prepared to react to aggression quickly and violently. As a black belt with 40 years of street experience, I have seen numerous people freeze when confronted by imminent aggression, yet jurors and the general public sit in their safe environments and question survivors' behavior. Why no injuries? Why no screaming? Why didn't they fight back? The Impact Phase of rape trauma and the body's reaction to trauma is why! Survivors are confronted by a situation they never believed would happen and where they have an overwhelming feeling of helplessness. Sometimes this helplessness is replaced by the feeling of confusion and blame due to the fact they were made powerless through alcohol or drugs.

People's reactions to survivors of assault can take many forms:
- **Distancing.** Female friends commonly listen to the survivor but then engage in behaviors that subconsciously separate the behavior of the survivor from their

own. Distancing psychologically insulates the friend from having to confront the very real thought that it could happen to them. For example: when a friend asks the survivor a question such as; "why did you let him take you home?" The friend is really saying to herself: "*I would never let that guy take me home, so this would never happen to me. I'm safe.*" Perhaps asking, "Are you sure it happened? You were really drunk and all over him." What the friend is now saying, is: "*I would never drink that much, and I surely would know what I was doing.*" Female friends frequently need to believe the survivor engaged in behavior that they would never engage in. This is setting the survivor apart and making what happened to her less threatening and real them.

• **Blaming.** "Why?" types of questions have no place in any conversation with a survivor. Understand he/she is already blaming themselves. More than anything else, they need you to empathize and show you believe them. It is not their fault. Simple questions such as: "Why didn't you tell me sooner?" Or, "why didn't you call me for a ride?" may seem rather harmless to you. What questioning does is point out something that cannot be changed. It is common to question the survivor's alcohol consumption or decision to wear clothing that is provocative. Questions like these only make the survivor feel even more responsible for what has happened. The survivor frequently apologizes because they did not do what others expect of them.

• **Revenge/Anger.** Often, males close to a survivor experience anger and feelings of revenging the wrong done to someone they care about. This macho, self-serving possessive attitude can frequently rear its ugly head. Many times, the first words out of a man's mouth are: "who did it?" Instead of showing genuine concern, anger and aggression take over. Survivors feel a responsibility to calm and soothe the male to prevent him from doing something stupid. Significant males must be supportive. Do not attempt to control the survivor or the situation. Bringing more violence into the situation will not help the survivor and will not cause the offender to change. Submerge your ego, listen, believe, and be patient.

• **Fixing.** Frustration and anger frequently drive significant others to do something to help. Actions such as calling the police or university officials without asking the survivor first, are all too common. Decisions being made without first talking with the survivor do nothing to help them regain the control that was lost and is now so important to them. Put the survivor first. Never take an action without their complete approval.-

• **Minimizing.** "It could have been worse." "He was cute, and you were drinking." "It was a week ago, get over it." "It's not like you were a virgin." These and many more insensitive statements are said to survivors every day. Perhaps the people making the statements think that by minimizing the assault it will somehow make it easier for the survivor. The reality is these people are using those statements to make the situation easier for themselves. Statements that minimize the assault do nothing for the survivor other than inflict further harm. Do not allow such statements.

The simplest and best advice is to listen, believe, and never ask a "why" question. There is absolutely nothing the survivor can do to change what has happened. The last thing a survivor needs is to have their actions questioned. What does it matter why they did not call for a ride, fight the man, or go to his room? The fact is they trusted the person and then were betrayed. It was not, is not, and never will be the fault of survivors. Behavior is a function of choice. The *survivor* made choices that **did not** include being sexually assaulted. The *offender* made choices that **did** include using whatever means necessary to get what he wanted. The offender is solely responsible for his behavior before, during, and after the assault.

Being there for the survivor means encouraging them to talk with someone trained to help them through this time. If the survivor is not ready you may want to contact an advocate or counselor for advice. Do not discount the effect this has on all who are close to them. Anger and helplessness are terrible emotions to deal with. This secondary trauma should not be ignored. It is hard to support someone else if you are not able to cope with your own emotions. Professional help is always encouraged for all parties.

What if the assault happened within the past few hours? What do I do? Rape crisis centers throughout the United States have established suggestions for someone who has been sexually assaulted.

• First, and foremost, attempt to make sure the survivor is in a safe location.

• Consider calling someone to talk to or be with the survivor. Advocate, friend, or both. The survivor needs someone they can trust.

• Medical needs must be considered. Injuries, pregnancy prevention and STI prevention options need to be addressed. Evidence collection is also an important consideration. The survivor may not want to report the assault right away, but it is possible she/he may want to in the future. Having evidence collected gives options if the survivor chooses. Look for a clinic or hospital that has Sexual Assault Nurse Examiners. They know how to effectively collect evidence while at the same time attend to the psychological trauma the survivor is experiencing.

• Legal and medical questions can best be answered by trained advocates. Look for one close. An excellent 24/7 national resource is RAINN (Rape, Abuse, and Incest National Network). Phone: 800-656-HOPE (4673) or their online chat is: online.rainn.org.

• Be sure the survivor goes at their own pace. Do not allow demands to be placed on them.

Survivors' needs must come first. No matter whom the survivor reaches out to or meets, their well-being must be the primary focus. Everyone deals with this in their own way. There is no right way for them to react. Everyone is different. Put the survivors' physical and emotional needs above all else. They may need to make sudden changes in their home, work or lifestyle to gain a sense of control and safety. The trauma resulting from what has happened can cause survivors to react in a variety of ways. They may feel numb and distant from others. They could want to forget what has happened but dreams and triggering incidents keep bringing it back. Seeking professional help can relieve some of these effects and help them begin the process of healing. Few of us are equipped to give anything but temporary support. Few of us could deal with this without feeling some trauma ourselves. Counseling provides a safe, private place for the survivor and those providing support to talk. Remember, never blame, never judge, listen, believe, and work to get professional help.

### REMEMBER
Sexual assault is a premeditated act with the intent of controlling and having power over another. It is not a mistake, a lack of communication, or somehow the responsibility of the target. Behavior is a function of choice. Predators, whether stranger or familiar, make a conscious choice to take something from another individual. To reduce your risk and avoid sexual assault, it is critical that you acknowledge that it can happen to you. It is also critical that

you play "what if." This involves rehearsing situations involving the "Nice Guy" and stranger. See yourself in potential situations and ask yourself what would you do if? Frequently, the difference between success and failure is preparation.

Knowing the basic characteristics of the "Nice Guy" and his behavior sequence gives you the knowledge to recognize when it is happening to you or people around you. Put yourself and friends' safety above worrying about hurting someone's feelings or being rude. Good men will not be offended. Never assume a man is good. Make people prove they are worthy of your interest and trust. Good men recognize the bad amongst them. Good men respect themselves and you. Good men recognize it is best when people give because they want to, not because they are forced.

The stranger rapist is rare but very predictable. He is looking for a target alone, generally at night in an environment with no people to support for witness. Look at your life and take reasonable measures to avoid situations where you have no support. Because we can't avoid all situations like these, carry yourself assertively and monitor your environment. Listen to your voice when it says you are uncomfortable. Don't deny it, identify why you feel that way. If something makes you uncomfortable, do what you can to get away from that environment. If confronted, maintain your assertive attitude and do what you need to do for yourself.

# THREE

# STALKING

*"Sometimes I unlock my car and find a rose on the seat –
no note, just the rose. Somehow, he got into my car and left
it there. It's all he needs to do to terrorize me."*

S talking is a problem affecting many in our society
today. Whether you are on a college campus, in a
rural community, or major city, it is very likely there
are people around you right now who are being stalked.
Approximately 1 in 4 women and 1 in 13 men will report
being stalked in their lifetime (14). Reports are far different
than actuals, so the numbers are likely much higher. Though
stalking has been present in our society for decades, it has only
been classified as a crime since the early 1990's.

California and New York were the first states to pass laws
making stalking a criminal offense. Since then, all states have
enacted laws making stalking behavior a criminal act. Though
each state words their laws differently, I have found a universal
definition to be: *a repeated and willful course of conduct
directed at a specific person that would cause a reasonable
person to feel afraid, intimidated, threatened or annoyed.*

If someone repeatedly follows or appears in your sight, approaches or confronts you in a public or private place, appears at your workplace or residence, enters or trespasses on your property, contacts you by phone, email, web site, perhaps sends gifts, or uses any other means of making their presence known that is unwanted, you are being stalked. The two critical words are reasonable and repeated. Would other reasonable people feel the same way you feel? Has the unwanted behavior, whatever it may be, occurred more than once? Let's assume the answer to both questions is yes, now what?

## IS ALL STALKING THE SAME?

An assumption made by many is that all stalking is basically the same. This may be true in legal terms and how it affects the targets, however, not all stalkers are the same, with the same motivations and behaviors. A strategy to deal with one type of stalker may not work with the other. I believe there are four basic types of stalkers.

### THE RESENTFUL STALKER

The most common is the person you dated exclusively who cannot accept that you no longer want to see them. They are upset by the breakup and may go to extremes to get you to come back to them. They are hurt, confused and believe themselves to be the victim.

*Katie dated John for several weeks their first year of college. Katie thought about ending the relationship, but when she would bring it up to John he would cry and beg her to stay. Finally, she decided she had to move on. The night she told John; he couldn't believe it. He thought they would be together forever. For several days, he would call to convince her to get back with him. She kept saying no. He would try to manipulate her with sympathy by saying he couldn't eat or sleep. Even threatening to kill himself as part of his manipulation to convince her to come back to him.* He needed her. *Though Katie never felt afraid of John, and in fact never labeled his behavior as stalking, she was dreading the calls and constant attempts to talk with her. One night, John became angry and stood outside her apartment screaming for her to give him another chance. The stress ended after Katie finally called the police. They told John to stop or there would be legal consequences.*

Though John felt like the wronged party, the Resentful Stalker needs a consequence to his behavior that will be sufficient to stop his obsessing. Police, student discipline, counseling or even a persistent friend could get him to stop. Though he has a loud bark, this one does not bite.

### THE DISCARDED STALKER

This stalker poses the greatest potential for violence. It begins with a long term, intimate partner relationship where one of the partners wants to end it. Though violence has been used by female stalkers, it is quite rare for a female to resort to violence against their partner. Watching the news around the country, most every time a woman is killed or presents herself to a hospital ER with injuries, she is the victim of domestic violence or a Discarded male stalker. Statistics involving the LGBTQ population show high incidence of being targeted by former intimate turned Discarded stalker as well. Whether their target is one who identifies as male or female, a male partner virtually always perpetrates the violence.

*Karen was a student at a Big Ten university. During her sophomore year, she met Kyle and became completely infatuated with him. They dated for a few weeks before deciding to move in together. Over the next several months, he became increasingly more possessive. She could not spend time with friends and had to account for all her time.*

*When she resisted, he would argue that he loved her and wanted her to spend time with him. It progressed to the point that he was putting her down in front of friends. She left him a few times but each time he threatened to kill himself, promised to change and begged her to return. Each time she returned, his controlling behaviors got more and more intense. He isolated her from friends and family. He sexually assaulted her repeatedly as a tool to achieve restoration of power in the relationship. She was finally able to break the bond and move away. Through repeated phone calls, texts and emails, he made statements such as "If I can't have you, no one will!" She involved the police and Kyle was charged with stalking. He is now on probation.*

I wish I had a good end to this story. Though Karen has moved and changed her name, she has the constant feeling that no matter what the police do, Kyle will not quit. Discarded stalkers like Kyle make headlines and wreak havoc with the lives of many. Do not ever assume stalkers are harmless. This is not always the case. The more intimate the relationship, the more likely the stalker will become violent. This is especially true if the stalker was physically abusive and forced sex during the relationship. This man feels a strong desire for revenge and control. It is important for roommates, friends, and family to take care and understand the possible threat he poses to them as well. Swift and firm law enforcement intervention is critical for safety.

## THE INCOMPETENT STALKER
This third type of stalker is not as likely to become violent, but the potential is always there. They are most likely to initiate contact with their target through social media.

*It began innocent enough; Jill had recently graduated and started work in a marketing firm. She was in a new community with no friends. As many people today do, she met someone through a service on the internet. They would chat regularly to the point where Jill felt she knew this woman. After a few weeks, they decided to meet in a restaurant. Jill enjoyed that first meeting and set up another dinner at her apartment for Andrea. Andrea arrived and they enjoyed their meal. They talked and laughed. The evening progressed to the point where Andrea expressed love for Jill and wanted sex. Jill was shocked and could not believe how quickly Andrea changed. Andrea grabbed her arm and told her, "you want me, I know you do." After much talk, Jill was able to get Andrea out the door. The next day, Andrea showed up at Jill's work and apologized. After Jill told Andrea to leave her alone, Andrea began screaming, calling her a "stupid lesbian bitch." Jill's coworker called the police. Jill has not seen Andrea since that day.*

This type of stalker interprets any kind of contact as an invitation. Unless law enforcement is involved, the Incompetent will continue to make contact. Fortunately for Jill, that cycle was broken by quick law enforcement intervention.

### THE DELUSIONAL STALKER
This final stalker is rare. They are complete strangers who have convinced themselves you are the one for them. They believe all they need is to approach you in person and you will quickly become attracted to them. They are very delusional, creating an elaborate fantasy of what will happen when they finally make this contact with you. The Delusional spends a great deal of time watching his target. It could be weeks or even months before they finally make contact.

*Allison was a gymnast attending a mid-sized eastern university. One day while crossing campus, a man approached, stopped her and commented on how much he enjoyed watching her compete. Broad daylight in the middle of campus, Allison felt initially comfortable speaking with him. They spoke and she thanked him for supporting the team. While speaking, he took out a binder from his book bag. He opened it to show her newspaper clippings he had collected of Allison. As she was becoming uncomfortable, he continued to turn the pages showing candid pictures he had taken of her coming out of practice, leaving her apartment and at social settings with friends. Allison said she "freaked out" and moved quickly away. He didn't expect that reaction. In his mind, once he showed her pictures and expressed how much he liked her, she would immediately want to spend time with him. Although truly strange, this happens all too often. She told her coach and the police. This man was soon apprehended, and counseling was mandated.*

Many movies over the past decade have romanticized stalking. Though to some it may be funny and harmless, predicting this behavior is difficult at best. Never underestimate the potential for violence. Always involve law enforcement.

## HOW DOES STALKING AFFECT THE PERSON BEING STALKED?

As you can imagine, the effects can be huge for people who are stalked, their friends, co-workers and family. People who have been stalked experience many different issues as a result of being stalked. Some of the more common are:

- Denial, self-blame, confusion, frustration

- Fear, anxiety, terror, isolation

- Irritability, hypervigilance, sleep issues

- Physical responses such as: headaches, fatigue, heart palpitations, eating issues

• Work and school problems such as tardiness, absence and productivity issues

• An inability to trust, which impacts relationships

• Financial problems caused by security measures, relocation, legal costs, time lost at work

Targets of stalkers frequently delay reporting through ignorance of the law, fear of retaliation, or confusion. They can't believe what is happening and have a difficult time classifying it as stalking. They may say the behavior is "irritating, but that can't be stalking;" "they show up all the time, but that's not stalking." To feel you have no safe place, always waiting for the next contact is exhausting.

## WHAT SHOULD I DO IF THIS IS HAPPENING TO ME OR SOMEONEONE I KNOW?

Avoiding a stalker is not always an easy or even possible solution. Simply attempting to avoid the stalker by not answering your phone or returning texts for example, one makes the erroneous assumption that no threat of violence exists, and as discussed already, this is simply not true. How can a person predict the behavior of a stalker? The answer is, they cannot make such a prediction. Because of this unpredictability, here are some successful options in the event you or someone you know is experiencing a stalker.

• Hold the stalker completely responsible. No one and no situation warrants being subjected to repeated stalking behavior. It is against the law and generally law enforcement intervention will cause the stalker to reevaluate their behavior. Involve law enforcement and/or campus officials as soon as possible.

- A frequent defense is for the stalker to say they simply did not know their behavior was not wanted. It is important to let the stalker know in no uncertain terms to stop. This can be verbally or written. The target does not necessarily have to deliver the message themselves. Friends, family, or court appointed individuals can help. For example, law enforcement can deliver a restraining order.

- If someone you were intimate with is stalking you, and if there was abuse within the relationship, it is critical that you have a safety plan before the police confront the abuser/stalker. Involve professionals immediately. Domestic violence hotlines are available to help connect targets of stalking with individuals trained to put safety plans in place.

- Document all incidents. Write down everything that happens, when, and the specifics of what occurred. It is important to record every detail including any witnesses. Too often survivors report, but when questioned by police they do not have specific information to help with the investigation. Day, date, time and specifics of the contact will help tremendously.

- Save everything! Texts, voice messages, letters, gifts, and any other concrete evidence you may have are important for obtaining restraining orders and reaching conviction.

- Inform those close to you about what is happening. Not only can they be witnesses, but they are also at risk.

- Follow through by doing whatever it takes to get the stalking to stop. This behavior almost never stops without legal intervention.

## *SOCIAL MEDIA STALKING AND HARASSMENT*

Cyber stalking and harassment are about power and control. Through phones and computers, cyber stalkers can gain enough information using social media to achieve their goal of manipulating their target into a face-to-face contact. Cyber harassers on the other hand generally avoid face-to-face contact. They get their power and control fix by disrupting a person's life anonymously.

*Sasha was a fifteen-year-old high school student when she first became aware of her cyber harasser. She posted some pictures of herself that she believed only her boyfriend would see. Unfortunately, someone she did not know was able to hack into the site containing the pictures. He posted her pictures and photoshopped other pictures to look like her. He created an incredibly pornographic web site using Sasha's full name. Not only was Sasha harassed by the harasser but also by others who found her through the web site. She believed her life was ruined. How could she get a job, knowing the first thing potential employers do is Google the name of the applicant? Embarrassed and defeated, she reached out for help. It took a very dedicated law enforcement officer to locate the harasser four states away and convince him to stop and remove the site or be prosecuted.*

Few people think bad things can happen to them. Fewer yet think it can happen through their computer or phone. It is incredibly easy for cyber stalkers to hack into sites and wreak havoc on lives.

- They may abuse you through personal contact

- As in Sasha's case they may set up web sites

- They may assume your identity

• They may access personal information, such as credit card information

• There is no limit to the creativity of these individuals to gain power and control by disrupting one's life

## WHAT CAN YOU DO TO REDUCE YOUR RISK OF CYBER STALKING?

The drastic answer is to basically go back in time twenty years! Knowing this is unrealistic, what are your options?

• Check privacy settings on all your accounts. With your social media sites, only allow information to be shared with friends or contacts. Privacy is critical to controlling your information.

• Do not have the same username for each site. Though this means you will need to remember a variety of names, this will make it much more difficult for stalkers to find you.

• Inform your friends if you are being stalked. Frequently, stalkers gain access to information through contacts. Hide all listings of contacts.

• Disable all location and tracking information on your phone. All someone needs to track you is your phone number.

• Close old accounts and delete them.

• Screen your calls by having them go to voice mail. Stalkers can "spoof" your phone by showing incoming calls and texts being from a false ID - someone other than the stalker.

- Change passwords frequently and keep computer security updated.

- Be careful accepting friends or requests. When in doubt, don't. Block people and accounts that you do not know.

- Make sure any online photo albums are private. Understand there is no guarantee, so be careful.

- Control tagging and being tagged. You give up control of privacy once you use tagging.

- Document all suspicious or overt contacts.

- Contact site administrators for support.

- Contact police.

- Never assume something or someone is harmless.

Understand that you do not know someone by communicating with them online. Predators are manipulative and will portray themselves as the greatest thing since sliced bread! Trust no one. I have worked many assaults where the target "met" the stalker online. After a period, the stalker would find a way to set up a meeting with their target. Sometimes they may get enough information to find the address of their target and show up unexpectedly. Several years ago, I consulted on a case in Michigan where a woman "met" a man on line. She believed he lived in Florida and was the owner of a very successful automobile dealership. He said he was divorced and was looking for someone he could talk with. After a few weeks of online talking, he showed up in her town. He called saying he was visiting a friend in a town close by and would like to take her to dinner. Knowing she lived alone, he offered to pick her up. He came over with a big smile and bottle of wine. Feeling she knew him well, she invited him in. Once the door closed, he became a predator. He sexually assaulted her, degraded her, and left with whatever money she had. She called the police. They attempted to track him through information he gave her as well as the IP address of his computer. All were bogus and the IP had been rerouted through Europe. He has not been caught.

## *"NO ZEBRAS" - BYSTANDERS AND STALKING*

You now know what stalking is. If someone you know is being subjected to this behavior what will you do? I hope the answer is support and help them. If you know someone engaging in this type of behavior, have the courage to take measures to get them to stop.

*When I was a college athlete in the late 60's, my girlfriend asked me to speak with one of my teammates, Jim, about his repeatedly calling her friend Anna. Jim went on one date with Anna and then proceeded to call her over 100 times throughout the next week to get her to go out with him again. Anna told Jim during the very first call that she did not want to go out with him again. I asked Jim if he thought that after the 99th call, Anna would suddenly see the light and agree to another date. His answer illustrates this type of stalkers mentality. He was sure she would say yes. He told me he loved her and wanted to convince her that she would love him too. I got the coaches involved who then got some help for Jim. It was crazy to me then, but now I know that stalkers do not always think like normal, healthy people.*

If someone you know is engaging in this behavior, suggest they get counseling or tell someone that can get them help. If you or someone you care about is being stalked, you would want people to do something, right?

### REMEMBER

Stalking is a criminal offense. Stalkers are usually intelligent, obsessive individuals who are self-absorbed. They want what they want and have no remorse for the trauma they are causing others. If is very difficult to reason with them. If you believe you or someone you know is being stalked, do not minimize it. Do not wait to seek help from the police or school officials. The sooner the behavior can be addressed and stopped, the better. The longer the behavior continues, the more obsessive the stalker can become. Do not fall prey to the attitude of assuming it will end soon if you just ignore it.

Stephen Thompson

# FOUR

# HARASSMENT

*"I hate going to work! People make comments about my appearance and laugh. I get called names and no one wants to talk with me, no one helps. It is just like high school."*

Does this person identify as a man or a woman? Does it matter? As uncomfortable as this material may be to read and think about, the fact is there are issues facing you that are not going to improve until we all become aware of them and choose to actively participate in making them better. A study published in Cosmopolitan magazine in 2015 found that approximately one in three individuals identifying as female in the United States will be harassed. Look at the news. Hardly a day goes by without a story of a politician, Hollywood personality, TV celebrity or corporate giant sexually harassing someone who works for them or someone they have power over. The studies of harassment with individuals in the LGBTQ community indicate over 61% experience some form of harassment. (15) Approximately one in four men in the workplace experience bullying/harassment. (16). Stories of harassment and bullying within social organizations and athletic teams are reported virtually daily. Regardless of the gender identification of the target, harassment is about one or more people feeling they have the right to exert power and control over another. Like sexual assault and stalking, power and control are the primary motives to harass and bully.

The dynamics around sexual harassment and stalking can be similar. In some cases, there is a very fine line between the two. Rarely is sexual harassment treated as a criminal matter when in the workplace or educational setting. In fact, the only time it can be treated this seriously is if the behavior escalates to the criminal level of sexual assault or assault/battery. Sexual harassment and general harassment are civil rights issues that are generally dealt with through Equal Employment Opportunity Commission (EEOC), Office of Civil Rights, Human Resources, civil litigation, or perhaps some other offices within your school or community. As with the definitions of stalking, definitions of harassment can vary from state to state. Although the behaviors may be quite different, the general definition of harassment is very much like stalking. Harassment is defined as *any behavior in a work or educational setting that would cause a reasonable person to feel offended, threatened, intimidated or afraid.* Where stalking is generally directed towards one individual, harassment can present itself in the form of a pervasive environment and/or behavior directed towards many different people. The Civil Right act of 1964 (17) established that when one is at work or school they have the legal right to be treated equally and fairly with dignity and respect, no matter the location or circumstance. If, because of gender identification, sexual orientation, hair color, ethnic background, social status, or other factors, anyone is treated in a way that would cause them to feel offended, threatened, intimidated, afraid and affects their ability to work or go to school, they are being harassed. What is at issue is how different entities deal with this rights violation.

Stephen Thompson

## *QUID PRO QUO SEXUAL HARASSMENT*

There are two basic types of harassment that effect people in the workplace or school setting. The first is called Quid Pro Quo, which is a "this for that" arrangement established by the harasser. A few of the more common examples would be: receiving a job promotion in exchange for sex; sex in exchange for better grades; keeping a job or getting a job in exchange for sex, such as the "casting couch" mentality the media has shown to be so prevalent in Hollywood. Sex is not the only criteria making the exchange a quid pro quo. Going on a date in exchange for better grades, or providing "selfies" in exchange for grades, job, etc., are other examples frequently seen. A high school student I helped several years ago is a classic example of Quid Pro Quo.

*Gail was living with her mom, going to high school and attempting to find a job that would allow her to afford college. A local fast food restaurant advertised job openings. She went to apply and while filling out the written application the manager approached her and asked a few questions. He looked at her application and told her that he wanted to interview her that night during the final hour of his shift. She agreed and came back later for what she thought would be a professional interview. The manager asked her why she needed the job as well as a little about her economic situation with her mother. The young lady became increasingly more uncomfortable with the manager. He finally told her that he had twenty people applying for the job; that he knew there were limited opportunities for her to get a job that would provide her the hours needed to get college money. He then told her if she wanted him to give her the job, she was to meet him at his car and "convince" him to hire her. She refused, left and told her mom. Angry and frustrated, the mom wanted this man punished. We were able to do just that by contacting the corporate offices and explaining the situation. The manager was fired within two days and the young lady was hired.*

I wish the majority of Quid Pro Quo types of harassment would end as positively, but unfortunately most do not.

*Take the example of Lindsay, who was an intern working for a state senator. Her life goal was to get her law degree and work in politics. The senator was aware of her goals and a meeting was set up to discuss the opportunity. During the meeting, the senator stressed how working with him would open many doors in the future. She was excited and expressed her appreciation for the opportunity. He concluded the meeting by telling her that he was divorced and wanted her to come to his house that night to relax and talk about her future. Though uncomfortable she agreed, believing he was a nice person. She went to the house that night. It did not take long for him to threaten that if she did not "sleep" with him he would make sure she would never work in politics. Confused and shocked she left. She reported the incident, but nothing was done. The conclusion was it was a "she said, he said" situation and the fact she went to his home indicated she was at fault.*

Too often targets of sexual harassment remain silent to avoid what Lindsay experienced as a result of speaking up: embarrassment, being shamed for 'not seeing this coming', and a lack of action."

Sex is the end product to the power and control that sexual harassers want to exert over their targets. Although most school and university faculty would not engage in this abuse of power, nor would most employers, those who do engage in this Quid Pro Quo behavior operate in an environment of secrecy. People who sexually harass feel entitled and above the rules. They operate from a position of power.

## Why Are So Few Cases of Quid Pro Quo Sexual Harassment Reported?

When a person is subjected to this kind of behavior, it often times starts slowly. The offender is in a position of power, and they work to reinforce the power differential while evaluating their intended target to see if they can get away with subtle inappropriate language and behavior. This could be a matter of hours or days. For instance, if the person in power is a famous movie producer, they would start by being very charming yet making sure their target is aware of the power they have over the target's career. They would talk about opportunities for the target while at the same time testing them to see if they can proceed to the next step of getting the target to an isolated location to make their demands. If the intended target were to refuse or confront the harasser the harasser will make one of two choices; they will either back down and attempt to convince the target this was all a misunderstanding, or they can intimidate with the quid pro quo. They will tell the target what will happen if they do not comply - reward and punishment strategy.

*Kim was a student in a senior seminar class at a western university. One day her professor struck up a casual conversation with her. He asked her about her plans after college. Over the next few weeks he was evaluating her by asking questions about her personal life. This is grooming behavior where he evaluates and plans the end game. He asked questions about boyfriends, drinking habits, her use of free time. All the while determining if she has the confidence to confront his inappropriate behavior and reject his advances. One conversation ended with him saying, "you have a great body, do you work out much?" The conversation made her uncomfortable and really bothered her, but she did not confront him nor ignore him by refusing to speak with him further. This was a major test designed by the offender to determine if he can proceed. She was not sure what to say or do. Two days later, he asked her to stay after class to talk about her grades. He pointed out his class was a requirement for her major and that she needed at least a grade of C to get credit and graduate. She couldn't believe this was happening. He told her they should meet later to talk about what she could do to graduate.*

This is classic predatory behavior. He picked out someone he felt he could exert power over, groomed her by appearing to be concerned, and then progressed to the quid pro quo end game.

What could have been done? The fact is that there are many people like Kim. They rarely report, why?

• Many are concerned that no one will believe them because of the stature of the offender; that they will be blamed and their motives for coming forward will be challenged.

• They hope the behavior was prompted by alcohol or some life stressor that is temporary and will eventually stop. They may try to evaluate the intent of the offender's actions, rather than accept the behavior itself as enough proof to report.

• Targets are groomed to the point that they are well aware of the power differential between themselves and the offender and of the ability of the offender to retaliate if refused. Targets are intimidated.

• Some are embarrassed by what has happened and want no one to know. Many women would feel embarrassed for the choices they made leading up to the moment they realized the offender's intent all along. Many people will perceive the woman's choices as naïve and foolish, and this is why the offender takes his time with the grooming process. When he is still grooming his target, the trust he instills in her gives her no reason to doubt him in the beginning. His patience provides more opportunity for his target to make choices she'll later feel ashamed and embarrassed to share openly.

• Many feel the process is more of a hassle than trying to deal with the harasser.

The truth is that schools, businesses and institutions want to have an environment free of this kind of abuse of power. It is bad public relations and can greatly affect productivity in the workplace. Unfortunately, power, status, and the ability to control others can be an incredible draw to some.

## HARASSMENT THROUGH OFFENSIVE OR HOSTILE ENVIRONMENT

This second form of harassment is the most frequently seen yet not as emotionally charged as Quid Pro Quo. Support for targets subjected to an offensive or hostile environment can be diminished. Statements such as, "Get over it," and "It's just a joke," are heard often when this form of harassment is reported. Examples of this form can be broken into four main categories. The first is **Visual:** suggestive or obscene looks, leering, gesturing, and displaying suggestive objects, pictures, cartoons, or posters that are offensive. Second is **Verbal** harassment: obscene or suggestive comments, inappropriate jokes, starting rumors, making sexual propositions, comments concerning the target's body, and pressures for dates are a few examples of verbal harassment. The third category is **Written:** this is seen where targets are receiving offensive letters, emails and notes. The final category is **Physical:** intentional touching, pinching, grabbing hugging, kissing, pinning someone or blocking their path are but a few examples of this. It is important to note that in some states these behaviors would be criminal sexual assault.

## Is It Harassment or Are Some People Just Too Sensitive? How Do I Know?

There are five criteria that should be applied to determine if the environment is offensive or hostile. This takes the guesswork out of it.

*1. Reasonableness:* would a reasonable person be uncomfortable with the behavior of the alleged offenders or environment? Is it reasonable others in the same demographics would be offended if subjected to that environment or behavior?

*2. Repeated or Pervasive:* though inappropriate behavior should not be excused, there needs to be repeated instances in order for a violation for the environment to be offensive or hostile.

*3. Effect vs. Intent:* the most common excuse given for this behavior is for the offender/s to say, "I was only joking around, lighten up!" It does not matter the intention of the offender. The effect the behavior and environment have on the target is the only issue. Does it cause the target to be uncomfortable, offended, or afraid? If yes, it is harassment.

*4. Avoidable:* if the offender/s or the offensive environment can be easily avoided with no inconvenience to the target, this is generally looked at as inappropriate; and most would argue that it is not harassment. However, for the most part, the behaviors and environment are not avoidable because they take place in the work or educational setting.

*5. Notice:* a defense to Offensive/Hostile Environment is for the accused to use the defense they simply did not know the behavior was offensive or inappropriate to the target. Offenders can sometimes argue that the target never said they were not ok with the alleged offender's behavior. Notice can be in written form, verbal, or even given by a third party to the offender. If the behavior or environment is brought to the attention of the school or business and is ignored, a Title IV or IX violation could be investigated.

## What Can We Do Now That We Know?

When ignored or not formally addressed, this behavior generally gets worse. Some targets of harassment attempt to defuse the harassment by "giving it back." This prompts many to believe that women are as likely to harass as men. I strongly disagree. This is done to conform with the group, and to fit in. One needs to ask if women generally initiate the offensive behavior or do they use it to retaliate as a defense mechanism? Defusing the situation by fighting harassment with harassment does not stop the behavior, nor does it create a more respectful environment. There are two avenues to deal with Sexual Harassment and Harassment within a school or business setting; Informal/Personal and Formal.

When addressing harassment through the Informal/Personal strategy there are two basic approaches. The first is called *Negotiation.* Think of this as a process where one would ask the offender/s to stop engaging in the offensive behavior. I use and recommend using what I call the **"XYZ Approach"**. Think of this as a form of mathematical equation where:

X = behavior that is offensive
Y = how the behavior makes you feel
Z = what you want to see happen

How does this work? Let's say a fellow student or co-worker named Tom makes rude comments to you. A negotiated response would be: *Tom, when you talk like that (X) it makes me feel really uncomfortable (Y). I do not want you to speak that way to me anymore (Z).* Perhaps you are in a situation where someone you work with or even a professor tells inappropriate jokes. *Professor Smith, when you make*

*jokes like that (X), it is offensive to me and others (Y). It is not appropriate, and I would like you to stop doing it (Z).*
If this strategy of **Negotiation** does not work, a second strategy you can move to is called **Confrontation.** The "**XYZ Approach**" is used again but this time you attach consequences to the Z. Using the previous example of Tom, you would use the same X and Y statement, but you change Z to: *I don't want you to ever say that again (Z)!! If you do, I will be forced to report you to.... (formal office on your campus such as Office of Civil Rights or workplace EEOC).* I have found that most harassment will stop being directed at you if you use **Negotiation** or **Confrontation.** If the Informal "XYZ" approach does not work, it is possible that if you bring the behavior to the attention of the offender's superior, such as a department chairperson or supervisor the behavior may stop. Unfortunately, the offender will direct the behavior to others that do not know what you know. Be sure to document what you have done to try to stop the behavior.
If the Informal/Personal approach to harassment fails, your next option would be the Formal approach. This involves submitting a formal complaint to the Office of Civil Rights on campus, the Human Resources and the Equal Employment Opportunity Commission if appropriate when work related. If they believe the complaint has merit an investigation will occur. The results of this investigation can take many forms from finding the complaint unsubstantiated and dropped to some form of consequence to the offender/s.
One final formal option would be to file a lawsuit against the offender and/or the entity where the behavior is occurring. This is a civil court issue where you hire and pay a lawyer to represent you. The downside to this is whether one can afford to obtain an attorney. Rarely will a lawyer represent a harassment case on a contingency basis.
With either the Informal or Formal approach, I recommend that everything is documented. Day, date, time, witnesses, other pertinent information, and the specifics of the

behavior should be documented. Without this, it may be very difficult to have action taken. It is unlikely you are the only one this person or environment has adversely affected. Through documentation and filing complaints, it is possible to reduce this kind of behavior in the academic or workplace setting.

### *"NO ZEBRAS"*

With the exception of Quid Pro Quo, I have found other people are generally aware of the Hostile/Offensive Environment yet do nothing unless they are directly affected. They laugh, they participate, they ignore but do not take it personally until it happens to them. It is certainly more comfortable to be in the group making the jokes and comments, than to be the one being made fun of and harassed. What if this was happening to you or someone you care about? What would you want to see happen? I am sure you would not want to see the "Zebra" mentality if help was needed.

What can you do?

• Speak with the target of the harassment and offer support

• If the offender/s are peers, X, Y, Z them. You add to their power by being silent, so tell them their behavior is offensive and to stop

• Inform supervisors; this can be done anonymously

• Look into formal resources and provide the information to the target

Once you notice the behavior, you have to make a choice. You can no longer say I didn't know. You always have three choices: participate, ignore it and make Zebra-like excuses, or take a positive action to address the behavior or environment.

### REMEMBER

With all sexual harassment, and bullying, behavior is a function of choice. No one makes a person sexually harass or bully another person. They are making a conscious choice. The law says we all have the right to learn and work in an environment free of this kind of behavior. Today more and more people are making excuses for inappropriate behavior. We are told that touching a butt, rude comments, "stealing a kiss" or other offensive behavior is either flirting or the offender is simply confused by the rules today. WRONG!! There is a huge difference between flirting and harassment. Flirting feels good for all parties and involves compliments that are legal and flattering. These compliments generally result in one feeling good and in control of the situation. Harassment is one-sided, involving comments and behaviors that are unwanted, degrading and generally resulting in one feeling intimidated, powerless, and upset. It is never the fault of the one being harassed. Don't ignore and be a Zebra. Take this issue personally and do something about it.

Stephen Thompson

# FIVE

# INTIMATE PARTNER VIOLENCE

*"It's going to take getting a bullet put in my head before people understand how serious this is."*

Violence within a relationship is different from other assaults because of the relationship between the abuser and the one being abused. This is not a crime involving a stranger who wants to harm you. It is not a crime where an acquaintance wants to harm you. It is a crime involving someone you trust and care for who is harming you. A betrayal by someone you have laughed with and shared experiences with. All too often, it can take the form of Elder Abuse where approximately 16% of elderly people are abused, mostly (76%) by people they once loved, family members (18).

*Florence, an 87-year-old widow, was living with her son and daughter-in-law. A few months into the living arrangement her son convinced her to sign all of her assets*

*and income to him so he could "use it to help with her care."*
*Shortly after that he started yelling at her for no logical reason.*
*He then started to restrict her to her room and even limited*
*her ability to speak with her friends. During a vacation he*
*took with Florence's money leaving Florence behind, she was*
*able to speak with a trusted friend about her fear and*
*mistreatment. This friend convinced her to speak with people*
*who would understand and help her. She is now living*
*happily and without fear in an assisted living facility.*

It can also take the form of abuse of people with mental
and physical challenges. This form is perhaps one of the
highest statistics, yet rarely talked about. Over 11% of all
young people abused are mentally and/or physically
challenged (19).

*Keenan, a fourteen-year-old Special Olympics athlete was*
*routinely punished by his parent/coach for not following*
*orders. Punishment consisted of being slapped, food being*
*withheld, and being locked in a closet. This abuse went on*
*for years until a social worker was able to intercede.*

Does this really happen here? Yes, here and everywhere.
Approximately one in three women and one in four men have
been abused by an intimate partner (20). The group most
targeted for this abuse are women between the ages of 18-24
(21). The primary reasons cited for relationship abuse in this
transition from adolescence to young adult time are: living
together without the marriage commitment, involvement in
casual sexual relationships, and multiple breakups and then
getting back together (22). Fifteen percent of all violent crime
is related to Intimate Partner Violence (IPV). This is the
leading cause of injury to women and is responsible for at least
8 million workdays lost each year (23). Think of the people
you know; the people involved in relationships. The
likelihood is that someone you are thinking about is in a

relationship that involves abuse. Unfortunately, it could be you.

## WHAT IS INTIMATE PARTNER VIOLENCE?

Generally, this violation can be described as: *a pattern of assaultive and coercive behaviors, including physical, sexual and psychological manipulation, as well as economic control that individuals use against their intimate partners. If a partner, spouse, boyfriend or girlfriend humiliates, insults, or swears at you, this is abuse. If they attempt to control your activities, threaten you, assault you, attempt to isolate you from your friends and family or tries to destroy your self-confidence and self-esteem, you are experiencing abuse.*

It starts innocently enough in most cases. The abusive partner is initially extremely attentive, putting their very best foot forward. Some experts call this time in the relationship the "Honeymoon" where everything is new and exciting. Controlling behavior is simply written off as love and concern. Eventually the dynamics progress to the point that one or more of the components of Intimate Partner Violence (IPV) surface in the relationship.

There are six specific forms or components of partner violence that though different, involve power and control either subtly or overtly. The typology of partner violence is outlined below with examples that help demonstrate each type.

Psychological/Emotional Abuse: Abusers break down their partner by chipping away at their self-esteem. Mind games, using the silent treatment by not speaking to them or ignoring them completely, putting them down while alone or with others, calling them derogatory names, non-verbal put downs through eye rolling, smirking, and body language cues are all forms of emotional abuse. A key part of the psychological and emotional attacks is in changing the rules and expectations. The abuser is in control and changes the "rules of the game" so the partner can never win or even break even.

For example, *Ann was in a relationship for over a year with Keith. During that time, Keith established expectations that changed frequently such as when they eat, what they eat, how she looked, and how to launder his clothes. One day dinner is supposed to be on the table at seven but the next day he demands it be ready by six.*

Keith created situations where he would get upset with her "incompetence" and "carelessness". These changes in rules and expectations by Keith were designed to keep Ann off-balance and him in control. No matter what Ann did, it would not be right. Keith, a Psychological/Emotional abuser, kept changing the rules of the "game", so that Ann could never succeed. This kept Keith in power over the situation and in control of the person.

Intimidation and Threats: Abusers use yelling to intimidate their partner coupled with angry looks and actions. They throw objects and smash things; especially property that is important to the partner. Abusers using this component will sometimes threaten to leave or to abandon their partner in a dangerous place if they do not get their way. A young woman I spoke with went on a weekend trip to Chicago with her boyfriend. During a discussion at a bar, he got upset with her and left. She was forced to pay the bill and find her way back to their hotel.

Jealousy, Isolation and Hyper Possessiveness: Some who are abused may associate jealousy with love. Relationship experts say jealousy is really a sign of insecurity. Abusers use it to control their partner by dictating who their partner can see, where they can go, and in what activities they can partake; all in the name of love and care. When the abuser is not physically with their partner in direct control it is not unusual for the abuser to call or demand that their partner call them frequently. Sometimes the abuser will unexpectedly drop by to observe their partner. Accusations of cheating on them are common.

It is threatening to the abuser to have their partner see family and friends. As the relationship progresses, the abuser allows fewer opportunities to see friends and family. Many times, they move away from family and friends. This is designed to isolate the partner and create more dependence. Ironically, it is also a sign of IPV for the abuser to manipulate their way into their partner's relationships with friends and family and use it as leverage when they may need it. Any manipulation with your relationships, whether separating you from, or involving themselves with friends and family in order to monitor and manipulate is a form of abuse.

Abuse of Privilege:  The abuser needs control through making the majority of decisions. They are the dominant force. Time spent together, where they live, the type of car they drive, are but a few of the decisions they control. Abusers feel they can do what they want, when they want; going out with friends and engaging in whatever activity they want but questioning and not allowing their partner the same freedom; a definite double standard. Abusers often control the finances and will complain about how much money the partner is spending. On the flipside it can also be abuse for an abuser to make the partner the one who has control over the finances, paying all the bills and making all the deadlines but then disregarding any spending controls.

A friend of mine shared this story. *My mom has always been solely "in charge" of the family's finances, BUT my dad gets to spend money on trips, booze, whatever he pleases but my mom can't spend too much at Target without enduring his drunken wrath.*

Sexual Abuse: Unwanted or uncomfortable touching or sexual conversation. Ignoring their partner's non-consent by forcing sex. It is common to see abusers treat their partners as sex objects to be used when they want. Sexual assault is common in abusive relationships.

Physical Abuse: This is frequently what people expect in partner abuse, the physical harm to the partner. You might see this starting with a simple grab of the arm to make a point. Then the behavior progresses to shaking, shoving and grabbing hair, and finally escalating to slapping, hitting, punching and other techniques designed to inflict pain.

### COMMON CHARACTERSTICS OF ABUSERS
Though situations are different, I have found some common traits of abusers. Most often abusers are men and or the dominant personality in the relationship. This person is typically very controlling, manipulative, having an attitude of entitlement and ownership. They are self-centered yet appear to outsiders as really nice.

Abusive relationships can be incredibly difficult to end. Because of this, knowing what to look for early on in a relationship can help oneself and friends/family with evaluating potential situations and possibly avoiding a bad situation before it progresses to the point of no return.

### "RED FLAGS" - BEHAVIORS THAT CAN INDICATE POTENTIAL ABUSERS
Are you or someone you know in a relationship where:
• the partner is resentful and jealous of time spent with friends and family?

• the partner thinks their feelings are more important than anyone else's?

• the partner has made threats?

• the partner continually makes changes in the "rules", creating anxiety and stress?

• there is reluctance to end the relationship due to fear of what the partner will do?

• compliance to keep the peace is more and more the course of action?

• the partner disrespects their partners' feelings by frequently making insulting comments and is critical of appearance, behavior, ideas, and virtually anything they can find to put their partner down?

If the answer to any of these questions is yes, a very critical evaluation of the relationship is in order. It is important to mention that many women stay because "not everything is bad" or "he can be so good" or "we have many great times". Many women choose to stay not simply out of fear for what he'll do if she leaves, but also because a part of her is so drawn to the "good" qualities he demonstrates and the "good" times they have. Part of "changing the rules of the game" is giving the partner good times at unpredictable times, leaving her wondering "when will he be like that again?". HOPE. For battered partners when every now and then the batterer is "wonderful, kind, affectionate" ... they have hope so the behavior of staying in the relationship remains constant.

### WHAT IF YOU FIND YOU ARE INVOLVED IN AN ABUSIVE RELATIONSHIP?

No advice is perfect because the dynamics of each individual relationship is different. You need to do what is right for you. I am told continually how hard it is to acknowledge that this is happening and even more difficult to end the relationship and leave. This is especially true if the abuser has isolated you from family and friends. You probably believe that you are somehow responsible and if you try just a little harder it will be okay. The reality is you probably love this person and cannot deal with the thought of being without them. It is common for this person to make you believe that no one else would want you. You and others probably make excuses for them by minimizing and denying much of what they do. It is important to understand their behavior is a function of the choices they make. Your partner is choosing to be self-centered, controlling, and abusive. You are not responsible for the choices they make.

What to do now? Trust your instincts. Is the voice in your head telling you things are not right? Instead of denying this voice, identify why it is talking to you. Confide in someone you trust. You will not be able to change your partner's behavior by changing your own. Realize the abuse will most likely not stop unless the abuser gets professional help. They must sincerely want to get help and change. It is never the responsibility of the battered partner to get help for the batterer. Even with professional help, there is no guarantee of change.

Make a plan and practice what you would do to get out of your residence quickly if they become aggressive. Have a safe place you can go. Know the resources available to you; legal advice, medical care, and counseling support.

### NO "ZEBRAS"!! IF YOU SUSPECT SOMEONE YOU KNOW IS EXPERIENCING ABUSE WHAT CAN YOU DO?

Violence and abuse do not just suddenly appear overnight. Obviously, if you or someone you know was screamed at or punched on the first date you would end it right then and there. The reality is this kind of relationship evolves over time. I have found that when dealing with individuals in an abusive situation there are things we should and shouldn't do. Above all, do not be a Zebra.

### Do:

• Let them know that you have noticed things that make you question their relationship, be specific.

• Express concern for them and reinforce the fact that the abuser is making a choice to abuse. That it is not their fault.

• Listen, believe, and support them without pressure.

• Check into resources for them, such as a place to stay, medical, legal, financial resources and counseling services.

• Be there for them unconditionally. It can take several attempts for them to end the relationship before the bond is finally broken.
• Be patient!

### Do not:
• Wait for them to come to you.

• Ask any "why" question. Such as, " *Why didn't you tell me sooner"?* These questions frequently make people who have been abused believe they are being judged. Why questions point at behaviors that have happened and can't be changed.

• Pressure them to make decisions. There is a difference between suggesting courses of action and telling them what to do.

• Place conditions on your support. Conditions such as; "*if you don't leave him, I'm done trying to help you."* Listening to someone who is being abused is very frustrating. Understand if you stop listening there may be no one else to offer support. However, abuse is a choice, but so is staying in an abusive relationship. Ultimately, what can a support person do after so long? What can a child do after so long of being endangered by an abuser when the other parent chooses not to leave? The harsh reality is there are few options other than ultimatums if all else has failed. *"Mom, I can't take it anymore, if you don't leave, I have to!"* One can hope it will not come to that.

• Take any action without their support other than self-preservation.

**REMEMBER**
Behavior is always a function of choice. No one asks to be abused and no one is responsible for the behavior of an abuser but themselves. Abusive relationships are everywhere; the room next to you, your home, the home of a friend, a co-worker perhaps. It is a pattern of behavior that starts with a courtship and ends with violence and abuse. Be aware, be educated, and be involved.

# SIX

# CHILD SEXUAL ASSAULT - WHAT ADULTS NEED TO KNOW

*"I can't believe he did this to my child! He was always so nice to Jason. Why didn't my son tell me sooner?"*

This quote from a parent is so typical of the response I hear. This quote embodies three critical issues when looking at child sexual assault. First is the disbelief that it could actually happen to them. Second is the belief that we would know a sex predator when we see one and that it would never be someone we know and trust. Third is the silence children have about what has happened to them. The purpose of including this part within the book is to address the fact that children can rarely protect themselves. It is up to adults to create a safe environment for children. To do this we need to understand the crime and the criminal.

## CALLING THE CRIME WHAT IT IS, THE SEXUAL ASSAULT OF A CHILD

Abuse and child molestation are the most common terms used in our culture to identify child sexual assault. I would argue that both terms minimize the severity of the crime. Think about it - of the following phases, which one impacts you the most? A child was sexually molested; or, a child was sexually assaulted, raped? Most would indicate the second statement, yet our culture seems to want to use the less descriptive terms of abuse and molestation. Why? I do not know the answer to that; however, I do know that the crime deserves the most impactful and accurate term to describe it and thus, in this book, we will call it child sexual assault.

## HOW HAS SOCIETY RESPONDED TO THIS CRIME?

Over the past decades we have all heard countless stories of the assault of children by sexual predators; priests, ministers, coaches, teachers, and famous billionaires to name only a few. In all cases there is outrage and a turning to the questions of why this happens and what can be done to protect our children? Why some deviant individuals, most likely men, sexually assault children is an issue better answered by psychologists. The fact is that they occur in numbers that are astounding, and social media is unknowingly helping to increase the numbers. Most experts I work with agree that it is unlikely that one can cure a pedophile (24). Pedophiles are defined as adults sexually attracted to children. It is important to understand that not all pedophiles physically act out with a child. Research indicates approximately six in ten pedophiles have had physical contact with a child (25) so it is best to assume they will act out if they have the opportunity. For those that have/would act out, the best one can hope for is to control them through incarceration or through counseling them to recognize what triggers them and to avoid the triggers.

The question of what we can do to protect our children is widely discussed and generally breaks down into two major strategies. The first strategy is to increase the penalty for harming a child. Punishing the predator makes us all feel we are doing something tangible to reduce the threat of child assault. Knowing they are off the street for the term of their sentence makes us safer from that specific predator. Laws giving convicted sex predators who assault children a life sentence for their first or second offense is a popular rallying point for politicians who want to show a strong stand to protect children. All states approach sentencing differently but all agree that it is a felony that carries with it the harshest of allowed penalties from months in jail to life in prison. Pedophile sex predators assault hundreds of children over their lifetime (26). The longer one is in prison, the fewer children he will be able to target. I am in favor of reasonable punishment; however, the problem with laws that are rigid is that they do not allow for variables such as age, and mental illness to name just two. For example, if a special needs person with a mental age of six commits a sexual assault on a six-year-old, should they be punished to the same extent of the law as a forty-year-old pedophile rapist? This example demonstrates the complexity of how challenging these incidents are to the legal system.

Interestingly, the threat of serving time in prison if caught is not a deterrent for offenders. The need to act out with a child is strong and the threat of getting caught rarely enters into the thought process of offenders. Most pedophile sex predators that I have interviewed and studied never believe they will be caught.

Convicting and incarcerating adults who sexually assault children is difficult at best. Why? To convict and ultimately incarcerate such adults means children have to be comfortable enough to tell someone about what was done to them. The someone they tell has to believe the child and report the crime. Law enforcement must then also believe the child and have the investigative training to be able to get a warrant to arrest the predator. To obtain a warrant the judge has to be convinced there is enough probable cause, which is not always easy when dealing with emotional parents and a silent child. Once caught, the prosecuting attorney must believe the child and have the knowledge to effectively prosecute and present a good case to a jury. Finally, the jury has to believe the child and ignore the reputation and status of the offender. This is all based on understanding the crime and the criminal who harms children. Generally, the child must take the stand in court... in front of the offender! If the child does not yet have the verbal capacity to explain what happened to them, this can also pose huge problems. If a child doesn't know the terms vagina, penis, etc. how can a parent or therapist help a child put the pieces of their assault together without risking accusations of "asking leading questions" or "concocting a story for the child to tell?" One major case I unfortunately know about involved a mother who fought like hell to protect her daughter from being assaulted by the child's father and grandfather. Because the marriage ended in a nasty divorce, this mother was "suspected of coaching her daughter into telling this story" in order to gain full custody. Even with mountains of evidence that included DNA, the jury still doubted the child was telling the truth.

The second strategy is to teach children about risk reduction and how to protect themselves. Books as well as experts attempt to teach children self-protection. Though emotionally satisfying in the thought we are doing something positive for our children, factually this rarely works. Risk reduction and self-protection will be explored in depth later in this chapter.

## WHO ARE THESE MONSTERS THAT ASSAULT CHILDREN?

There are several different profiles of offenders who sexually assault children. However, we will focus on the one most responsible for the vast majority of sexual assaults of children. I have termed this prolific predator the" Preferential Seductive Child Rapist". Their most apparent and common characteristics are:

• He is intelligent and most likely a college grad with a good job.

• He assaults for years; leaving a trail of damaged children behind.

• Unlike other sexual predators, the Preferential will continue generally for the rest of their life unless caught, meaning there is no specific age range.

• He is addicted to the fantasy and reality of assaulting a child. Much like how a drug addict is consumed with getting their next fix, the Preferential is continually working towards acquiring images of children or children themselves.

• His addiction drives his behavior. He must be in a position to be around and evaluate children. Think of jobs and volunteer settings where he can be around children. This is *not* to say that people that are in jobs and volunteer situations with children are Preferentials; it is to say that Preferentials will definitely gravitate towards those settings.

• He is well organized in his daily life and in his quest to target children. He does not operate impulsively. He thinks ahead and is quite calculated.

• His preferred target are young boys.

• He can be a well-respected community member, making him less likely to be suspected.

• He may be married but will likely have sexual problems with adults.

• He will demonstrate signs of his fixation on children at around the age of 16 .

• *He is* Tooooooo.......everything! Too quick to volunteer to chaperone dances, field trips, playgrounds. Too nice, making it too easy to ignore suspicions.

• He can/will assault an average of 250 different children in his lifetime. Some known offenders have assaulted well over 1,000 different children. (27)

### HOW DO THEY SO EASILY SUCCEED?

Much like sex offenders who target adults, predators who target children follow an identifiable behavior pattern that is consistent and predictable. The Preferential Seductive Child Rapist's assault sequence involves a clearly defined four-step process.

Step 1:  *Target Selection.*

He works in or frequents an environment that includes children so he can pick and choose, hunting for the ones he feels best meet his criteria. Are they leaders of a group or are they on the fringe of the group? Do they seek the attention of the offender? While looking for potential targets, he is also scrutinizing the parents or guardians. He prefers children whose parents are not so involved with the lives of their child; parents too busy or preoccupied to come to school functions, games, or important activities. Examples would be parents who drop their child off at practice, never watching practices and frequently being late to pick them up.

### Step 2: *Evaluates and Grooms*

This is the predator's method of gaining the child's trust to ensure the child won't tell anyone. Will the child eventually trust him without telling? He is extremely nice, attentive, complimentary and above all sees that the child craves his attention. He will spend time cultivating the relationship gaining more trust, while learning about the child's relationship with their parents. At this stage in the process the predator will be creating situations where he can be alone with his intended target. In these moments alone with the child, he will be testing his choice by slowly engaging in inappropriate language and behavior. Does his prey confront, and if so, can the predator easily explain away the behavior?

### Step 3: *Sexual Violation.*

If there is little or no resistance the predator will eventually escalate to the overt sexual violation. The child is conflicted while being intimidated by the position of power the predator has over him. The predator generally begins with fondling and eventually escalates into other violations. Guilt, shame, betrayal, helplessness, confusion and fear are but a few of the emotions the child will feel during and after each violation.

### Step 4: *Termination.*

The goal here is for the predator to leave the child feeling that no one will believe their story and that the child wants this and that the price of silence is to continue being in the predator's favor. The success of the predator cannot be overstated. It is very rare for the child to ever tell and if they do, it can be years later after they have endured the psychological aftermath to the point that they cannot remain silent.

## WHY ARE CHILD SURVIVORS SO SILENT?

The trauma that adult survivors of sexual assault experience is generally extremely intense and life altering. Imagine a child, who has their whole life ahead of them with eyes wide open, trusting and being dependent upon adults. Imagine what must go through a child's mind when their belief system and trust are betrayed. Their behaviors during, immediately after, and long term vary; however, not telling anyone is very consistent with child survivors in general. Children's minds do not process information and trauma the same way we as adults do. Thus, we cannot explain or predict with our adult minds the mind of a child who has been sexually assaulted.

There are many reasons for children being silent when they are assaulted. They include:

• Being confused. It may feel good, but they know it is wrong.

• Too young to articulate.

• Fear because the offender may threaten to harm them or their family.

• The offender may bribe the child with a quid pro quo arrangement. He will give them something in exchange for the sex he wants.

• Fear they will not be believed by adults.

• Children may blame themselves for the behavior of the adult.

• The child may feel ashamed/stupid.

• The child may not want to get the abuser in trouble. Many times, the abuser is someone the child loves. A parent, a sibling, etc. This can be another major contributor to feelings of confusion.

• The child may feel isolated and believe that they cannot trust anyone.

Too often adults deny that this crime could happen and dismiss the child because they cannot deal with the reality that it happened. Adults may convince themselves that the child is lying and influenced perhaps by a television show or others to falsely accuse in order to get attention.

## CHILD CENTERED RISK REDUCTION AND SELF-DEFENSE

As was written earlier, the question of what can we do to protect our children is widely discussed and generally breaks down to two major strategies. We addressed earlier the strategy of increasing the penalty for harming a child. Let us now address the other strategy, the belief that children can be taught to reduce their own risk and defend themselves.

When looking at this issue the majority of books, web sites, and experts speak to either children protecting themselves from bullies, or attorneys giving advice to deal with child assault accusations. There is little fact-based information concerning risk reduction available. The fact is that general advice given today to children involves tactics such as not talking with strangers, don't open your door to people you do not know, and other pieces of advice that addresses "Stranger Danger". The main issue is that rarely do strangers attack children. When they do, the motives and outcomes are generally way beyond what we can prepare children for. The greatest risk comes from someone the child knows; the person who gains the trust of the child. As was shown earlier, these predators put themselves into positions where they are around children so as to have an abundant source of potential targets. They select the ones they want and then take their time gaining their trust and grooming them to be compliant and ultimately silent.

As was stated earlier, predators will rarely select a child that they believe to have a close relationship with their parents. Children from split homes, abused children, and children that are in dysfunctional settings are most often the ones selected. It is rare for a predator to select a child that has involved parents from a functional home or homes. Predators do not want to contend with the variable of disclosure.

So, what is the answer to risk reduction and self-defense for children? What our culture does not generally talk about is that it is our responsibility as adults to create an environment where Preferential Seductive Child Rapists cannot easily access children. It is our responsibility! No matter how smart and streetwise we think our children are, they are generally unable to protect themselves from this type of predator. So, if incarceration is not a deterrent, and teaching risk reduction and self-protection is not greatly effective, what do we do?

## WHAT CAN ADULTS DO TO PROTECT CHILDREN?

To help children, we need to be attentive and proactive. Much like a slug on a sidewalk that leaves a trail of slime Preferential Seductive Child Rapists generally leave a trail as well. Look for the trails.

Pedophiles that do not physically act out with children can be in an office, court setting, or a multitude of jobs. Whereas the pedophile rapist must be in jobs and settings where they have regular access to children. They may show multiple changes in jobs. It is common for schools, churches and hospitals to send suspected offenders away with a letter of recommendation rather than confronting the offender. The excuse for this is that they are afraid the offender will sue and bring negative publicity upon the entity.

All too often we are passive bystanders making excuses for the predator and being skeptical of the target. Never assume someone is trustworthy when relating to our children. Drop in at practices, church functions, etc. Observe and be involved. Speak with parents when you feel uncomfortable. Listen to the "voice" in your head when something does not seem right. Talk with your child and create an environment where they can disclose their feelings. Above all, listen and believe. Do not deny, make excuses and minimize. Tell authorities if you suspect someone is targeting children. Report offenders, press charges and support those who do. Though we will not be able to change this predator, it is possible we can limit his ability to harm children. Additionally:

- Acknowledge the "who" and "how" of predatory behavior.


- Establish community alliances with schools, churches, community counseling and law enforcement.


- Prosecute


- Hold school administrators responsible for doing background checks and being observant. Do they regularly drop in on practices? Do they regularly evaluate and observe playground supervision, transportation people, crossing guards and anyone else having contact with children? Do they listen or do they ignore?

### REMEMBER
At the beginning of this chapter I said there are three critical issues when looking at child sexual assault; first, is disbelief that it could actually happen to your child. Now you know that it **can** happen to any child. Child porn was once

very difficult to attain; however, the internet has now made it available to the extent there are thousands of web sites. These sites feed the addiction and can trigger some to cross the line from consumer of child porn to predator.

Incredibly popular, social media sites are used daily to access children. Our home is the place we feel the safest, yet every day our homes may be infiltrated by predators targeting our children. To address this and reduce risk, the Innocent Lives Foundation (28) advises parents to set their children's profiles to private and to teach them to:

- NEVER accept friend requests or follow requests from strangers and why.

- NEVER share personal information or photos with strangers online

- Only chat online with people you know in real life

- Never meet strangers from social media in real life
Parents, do not hesitate to monitor your children:

- Keep up with their online behavior

- Control privacy settings to make sure your children have private accounts

- Set controls that prevent your child from accepting friend requests without your permission

- Obtain your child's passwords and check their accounts often

The second critical issue is the belief that we would know a sex predator when we see him.

Stop in on activities and observe. Above all, never ignore or minimize Most of us feel we are good judges of character; however, as was shown, the sexual predator could be the nicest person you know. We attempt to prepare our children for "Stranger Danger" but do little to prepare them for the trusted adult who is their coach, teacher, priest, bus driver, playground supervisor, or family friend. Evaluating adults that are around children simply means being involved. Were background checks done on coaches, youth leaders, and school workers? Don't assume! Ask the school to provide these answers. Hold them accountable for providing a safe place for your children. Above all, never ignore or minimize the voices of children.

The third critical issue regarding child sexual assault is the silence children have about what has happened to them. Parents would like to believe their child would resist and then quickly tell them of what has happened. I wish that were true but as we know, children rarely tell immediately after being assaulted, if ever. The reasons are complicated for the adult mind to comprehend but make perfect sense in the child's mind. It is up to us as caring, informed, and vigilant adults to protect children. They are rarely able to protect themselves.

# No Zebras!

Stephen Thompson

# A FINAL WORD

# ONE VOICE

T his book has been written for you to use in gaining an understanding of the complexities of sexual aggression by focusing on five main areas: 1) Sexual Assault; 2) Stalking; 3) Harassment; 4) Intimate Partner Violence; and 5) Child Sexual Assault. This information, and how you can make a difference, means nothing if you do not take it personally by acknowledging that this issue affects you and the people you care for. I frequently hear people making the excuse of doing nothing about sexual aggression because they are only one person, one voice and what difference could they make? Historically, the fact is that it has been simply one voice that has created change in the area of sexual aggression. Examples such as:

*In the mid 1990's a little girl was sexually assaulted and killed by a predator that lived close by. Her mom, Maureen Kanka, wanted to know why she was not made aware that a child rapist lived so close. At that time there were no laws concerning sex offender registration and notification. Ms. Kanka lobbied her legislators in New Jersey and persevered to the point that a law was enacted that required all sex offenders to be registered. Today all states have sex offender registration. One person, one voice had a positive effect on the safety of children by not settling for excuses.*

*In Florida, one nine-year old's voice spoke from the grave through her father to lobby legislators to have mandatory jail sentences for sex offenders who harm children, so no child would suffer what little Jessica suffered at the hands of a repeat offender. Jessica's predator would have been in jail after his first assault, not on the street to harm another child if this law were in effect. Today all states have mandatory sentencing for repeat offenders but more needs to be done.*

*The "Me Too" movement began in 2006 by one voice, Tarana Burke. She used the words initially on social media to bring attention to sexual harassment and to empower women through empathy and strength in numbers, especially young, vulnerable women. She accomplished this by visibly demonstrating how many women have survived sexual assault and harassment, especially in the workplace. The "Me Too" movement has grown today to huge proportions.*

*A final example is the voice of Rachel. Rachel was the first survivor to have the strength to come forward and accuse her sports doctor of sexual assault. Her single voice spurred hundreds of other Dr. Larry Nasser survivors, to speak out. Once voice empowered many other voices resulting in great changes in the way universities and colleges respond to the voices of survivors.*

Your voice can be heard as well, whether it is to people close to you, or to strangers you may come in contact with through your profession or interests. To be effective you need to remember some of the key elements of the book.

<u>Judgement vs. Responsibility;</u> no one ever asks to be assaulted, stalked, harassed or harmed by an intimate partner.

Offenders are 100% responsible for their behavior regardless of the behavior of their target.

Premeditation: a word most do not hear in relation to sexual aggression. Many want to believe these behaviors are impulse driven caused by alcohol, or the survivor. Rarely is this the case. Most sexual aggression involves planning, and prior thought. Whether a stranger or someone known, offenders think, they fantasize, and they plan what they are going to do to their target. This behavior is no accident.

Sexual Assault affects at least one in four women, one in ten men, and countless children. It is defined as anytime, anyone does anything of a sexual nature where there is no consent. Getting a person under the influence or targeting someone who is already under the influence of alcohol or drugs is against most state laws. "Nice Guys" are responsible for the majority of sexual assaults. There is a big difference between "Nice" and Good. Never assume!

Stalking is any repeated behavior that causes a reasonable person to be afraid, intimidated, or offended. The more intimate the stalker has been with the target, the more likely violence will occur. Never ignore this behavior as it rarely ends well without law enforcement intervention.

Harassment, whether at work or in a school setting is a civil issue and generally a violation of federal Civil Rights Laws. Everyone has the right to be treated equally, fairly, and with dignity and respect. If a person is subjected to offensive, repeated behaviors that affect their ability to work or be a student, it is wrong, no matter what the excuse.

Intimate Partner Violence can affect up to thirty percent of long-term relationships with the statistics going higher with some populations. No one has the right to abuse their partner, whether emotionally, economically, or physically.

Child Sexual Assault is a silent epidemic affecting children, families and institutions. Education and involvement are critical to identify offenders and restrict their ability to target children.

No Zebras. Albert Einstein once said, *"the world is a dangerous place, not because of those who do evil, but because of those who stand by and do nothing about it."* This is the heart and soul of bystander engagement and the Zebra Philosophy. Most aggression happens in situations where other people either see it happening or are aware of it, yet they ignore it and do nothing. We make excuses for our inaction. Understand it is an excuse that can result in others being harmed. Take this issue personally! It takes courage to confront our own ignorance and bias. It takes courage to perhaps admit there were times we made assumptions that now we see were wrong. It takes courage to step up when needed instead of stepping down. How do you want people you care about treated? That is the standard we should have with all aspects of sexual aggression.

One final voice is that of Gandhi... *"You must be the change you want to see."*

# References

1. Association of American Universities (AAU) Climate Survey on Sexual Assault and Sexual Misconduct, (2015, September 3).

2. Black, M.C., Basile, K.C., Breiding, M.J., Smith, S.G., Walters, M.L., Merrick, M.T., Chen, J., & Stevens, M.R. (2011). The National Intimate Partner and Sexual Violence Survey (NISVS): 2010 Summary Report. Atlanta, GA: National Center for Injury Prevention and Control, Centers for Disease Control and Prevention.

3. Ibid

4. Williams, K.S. and Bierie, D.M. (2014). An incident-based comparison of female and male sexual offenders. *Sexual Abuse: A Journal of Research and Treatment, 27*(3), 235-257.

5. Truman, J. and Langton L. (2015, August). Criminal Victimization, 2014. Department of Justice. Office of Justice Programs Bureau of Justice Statistics.

6. Lisak, D; Gardinier, L; Nicksa, S; Cote, A. (2010). "False Allegations of Sexual Assault [sic]: An Analysis of Ten Years of Reported Cases". *Violence Against Women.* 16(12),1318-1334.

7. Ibid

8. Morgan, R.E. and Truman, J.L. (2018, December). Criminal Victimization, 2017.Department of Justice, Office of Justice Programs, Bureau of Justice Statistics.

9. Ibid

10. Hale, M. (2002). *The History of the Common Law in England.* University of Chicago Press.

11. Cherry, K. (2019). *History and Biography; Freuds Perspective on Women.* Very Well Mind.

12. Thompson, S. (1995, May). Date/acquaintance rape: The crime and criminal profile. *Campus Law Enforcement Journal*, 25 (3),21-22, 36.

13. Long, J. (2006). Explaining counterintuitive victim behavior in domestic violence and sexual assault cases. *Voice*, 1(4), 1-3. American Prosecutors Research Institute, National Center for Prosecution of Violence Against Women.

14. Black, M.C., Basile, K.C., Breiding, M.J., Smith, S.G., Walters, M.L., Merrick, M.T., Chen, J., & Stevens, M.R. (2011). The National Intimate Partner and Sexual Violence Survey (NISVS): 2010 Summary Report. Atlanta, GA: National Center for Injury Prevention and Control, Centers for Disease Control and Prevention.

15. Human Rights Campaign. (2013). Growing Up LGBT in America: HRC Youth Survey Report Key Findings. Washington, D.C.

16. Namie, G. (2014, February). U.S. Workplace Bullying Survey. Workplace Bullying Institute.

17. The Civil Rights Act of 1964, Pub.L. 88–352, 78 Stat. 241, (1964).

18. National Council on Aging. Elder Abuse Facts. https://www.ncoa.org/public-policy-action/elder-justice/elder-abuse-facts/

19. Smith, N. and Harrell, S. (2013, March). Sexual Abuse of Children with Disabilities: A National Snapshot. Center on Victimization and Safety, Vera Institute of Justice.

20. Brown, S.L. and L. Bulanda, J.R. (2008). Relationship violence in young adulthood: A comparison of daters, cohabitators, and marrieds, *Social Science Research*, 37 (1), 73-87.

21. National Institute of Justice. Office of Justice Programs. (2017, August 27). Relationship Abuse During The Transition From Adolescence to Young Adulthood.

22. Ibid

23. Ibid

24. Seto, M.C. (2009). Pedophilia. *Annual Review of Clinical Psychology.* 5, 391-407.

25. Carey, B. (2019, September 29). Preying on Children, The Emerging Psychology of Pedophiles. New York Times, https://www.nytimes.com/2019/09/29/us/pedophiles-online-sex-abuse.html.

26. Lanning, K.V. (2010). Child Molesters: A Behavioral Analysis. National Center for Missing and Exploited Children.

27. Ibid

28. Innocent Lives Foundation. How Predators Have Infiltrated Social Media. https://www.innocentlivesfoundation.org/how-predators-have-infiltrated-social-media/

# About the Author

Mr. Thompson is one of the nation's leading experts on the topic of sexual aggression. His experience includes:

- Sexual Aggression Services Director and tenured university professor, retired after 42 years
- Presented several hundred programs and trainings on the topics of sexual assault, stalking, harassment and partner violence, throughout the world to universities, corporations, military enlisted, and military command staff.
- Court Qualified, Expert Witness - Counterintuitive Behavior, Sexual Assault, Stalking, Dating Violence
- Worked with U.S. Senate subcommittee to establish peer advocacy in all military installations
- Sex crimes investigation trainer, consultant, and criminal profiler
- Sexual aggression advocate trainer••
- Threat assessment consultant
- Researched and published the first and most comprehensive date rapist profile and behavior sequence called the **"Nice Guy"** (Campus Law Enforcement Journal, May 1995)
- Author of <u>No More Fear,</u> 1996, Kendall/Hunt, Dubuque, Iowa, 1999

- Started the first university peer-to-peer sexual aggression confidential advocacy program in the nation that serves as the model advocacy program today
- Wrote, directed, and produced the program and DVD, *"No Zebras, No Excuses, Addressing the Bystander Mentality"*
- Former college athlete and coach
- Black belts in Hapkido and Judo
- Owner: No Zebras & More LLC. For further information, please contact www.nozebrasandmore.com

Made in the USA
Columbia, SC
22 June 2020